THIS IS
MINUTEMAN
TWO-THREE... GO!

THIS IS MINUTEMAN
TWO-THREE... GO!

MEMOIRS OF A HELICOPTER PILOT
IN VIETNAM, IRAQ, AND AFGHANISTAN

WAYNE CHASSON

HUEY
BOOKS

For information about special discounts for bulk purchases or author interviews,
appearances, and speaking engagements please contact:

Wayne Chasson
wayne.chasson@gmail.com

First Edition

Edited, cover, and book design by Rodney Miles, www.RodneyMiles.com
Cover image by WikimediaImages from Pixabay

CONTENTS

PREFACE

A S MISSION REQUIREMENTS started to wind down while flying in Afghanistan, I was faced with longer flight times between landing zones. To help pass the time I started jotting down notes of my six decades of flying, just a hodgepodge of flashbacks. At the end of the day, back in my hooch[1], I would try and put the hodgepodge in some kind of order. At first it was just rambling, then as I got farther into it the notes became almost therapeutic. Some memories would come pouring out, some I just held back until I was ready. Soon, I had some *two hundred and fifty pages.*

I had no illusions of the end result. I wasn't sure if I was writing this for myself or maybe my grandchildren. I never really thought anybody would be interested in what I had to say. As I said, it really started out as a way to eat up time between landing zones or FOBs[2]. If you've gotten this far, maybe the title or pictures got your attention. If so, thank you getting this far. I hope you can enjoy and feel part of my six decades of aviation. As of today it's been fifty years since I stepped off the Boeing 707 in Vietnam. There is more than a little dust

---

[1] (hooch) plywood huts that housed the aviators in the base camp in Vietnam (see Glossary in the back)

[2] (FOBs) forward operating bases

on the bottle, not to mention my hair. My memories have aged with time but still the flashbacks remain vivid, even if only for a moment.

Stories are arranged chronologically and grouped by stages of my military and civilian career. Please note that for your information and better enjoyment of the text, in the back of the book there are sections that briefly discuss the Huey as well as a glossary for clarity on what is being said and immersion into the world I've been a part of and *survived*.

And if nothing else, in the back of the book, please read "The Wall." All gave some, some gave all.

Wayne Chasson

West Palm Beach, Florida

November 2019

PART 1:

In Country

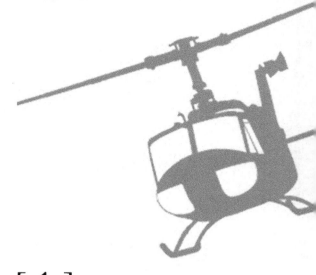

[1]

DAY ONE

MY MEMORIES MAY have faded with time, but not my recollection of that first day in Vietnam. Throw some diesel fuel on a bucket of human waste and you have a scent that will live in your memory forever. That's what I remember most about my first day—the smell. That and the air, or the lack of it. Disembarking from the plane, we were greeted by a pungent stench that could only come from a combination of heat, humidity, and burning feces from the outhouses. Right there at the doorway of the Flying Tiger 707, it felt as if all the air was being sucked out of my lungs. My mind leapt to early lessons from flight school: "Lift and Bernoulli's Principle"—nature abhors a vacuum; high pressure always overtakes lower pressure. Could there be a lack of oxygen in Vietnam? That was it—the air in my lungs was going to replenish the air in this stinking country.

Making my way down the stairs, I wondered what was next. *Can I wait right here for the war to be over, or will someone have a plan for me?* A sergeant calling out, "Newbies form over here," soon answered that question. Rank made no difference, all newbies were lumped together, which was fine. I didn't want to stand out. Two large duffle bags came off the plane, and there I stood, 9,000 miles from home, a day earlier than when I had left.

I have learned there are four "o's" in life, all fairly self-explanatory: First is "Oops." This is the easiest to resolve. Next is "Oh no"—a little harder to overcome, but again no worries. More serious is "Oh shit," which isn't the end, but it can be a game-changer. You must be careful: you never ever want "Oh shit" to become "Oh fuck" because those are almost impossible to recover from. This definitely felt like an "Oh shit" moment.

What was I doing here? How did I get here?

[2]

From "Oops" to "Oh Shit"

LIFE WAS GOOD: I was in love with Aileen, I had my license, and my parents were great. Aileen was the girl I was destined to marry. She had a face that could stop a clock, a dark-haired beauty with Bette Davis eyes that mesmerized you. More importantly, she had a laugh that was infectious. She was never afraid to laugh at herself. My dad worked endless hours as the owner of a small dry-cleaning business but found time when he could to be involved in school and sports. My mom worked but arranged her job to be home as we went off to school and more importantly to be there when we got home. She wanted the best for us even though financially it was difficult. For example, she loved the idea of us playing golf. A full set of golf clubs was out of the question but a seven iron and a putter would do, for starters.

I was a typical high school student with average grades from a school with one of the top reputations in the country. Newton, Massachusetts was everything a boy in his teens could want—or at least this boy. I thought I was destined to have a good life with no worries or cares. Tomorrow would take care of itself. As a seventeen-year-old starting senior year, I didn't pay much attention to the news. It was September 1964. I would just ride the wave with the Beach Boys in the background, waiting for a "plan" to unfold. Fall rolled into winter, and then suddenly it was spring. Oops—would I get into college?

Things were heating up in Vietnam, but how could something on the other side of the world affect me? I knew that if I didn't go to college I could be eligible for the draft. But I wasn't yet eighteen and didn't have to register for the draft for the time being. I had plenty of time to get ready for college, I thought. But when all the schools I applied to turned me down, I had my first, "Oh no."

I threw in with a college pool, and the University of Pittsburgh was willing to take a chance on me. Unfortunately, the university also said I had to go to a summer program in Johnstown as a trial run, to ensure I was college worthy. If I was successful there, I could move on to the main campus in Pittsburgh.

I kissed Aileen goodbye, saying, "Wait for me. I'll be thinking of you every day." She assured me she would miss me terribly. Then off I went to Johnstown, PA. Up to this point, I had barely ventured out of Massachusetts, but here I was in the middle of nowhere. The University of Pittsburgh summer program was easy. Most of the initial classes picked up with material from the middle of senior year in high school. I started off with a bang, earning A's and B's in everything. I figured this college thing wasn't going to be that hard, and I could devote my life to girls and goofing off. In fairness to Aileen, whom I would talk to at least once a week, I didn't date any girls, but I was an excellent flirt (one of my few real talents). But the pace at which the professors taught in college was much faster than in high school, and it didn't take long for my A's and B's to drop to C's and, by the end of the summer, D's. Another "Oops," but with the potential to become another "Oh no."

In order to secure the move to the main campus in Pittsburgh, I had to ace the finals. Exams came, and the results were plain: the University of Pittsburgh said it was "not the right time" for me to continue. My "Oh no" moment was racing toward becoming an "Oh shit."

Fortunately, back home was Newton Junior College, though it was not exactly what I had envisioned. I was no longer a cool kid going to a big-name university. I was, however, back to living the good life. Junior college was full of kids who didn't or couldn't get in to college, either from poor grades or lack of money. I quickly bonded with them, and, of course, there was still Aileen. She was now a senior in high school so we had the rest of our lives together. The fall of 1965 felt like a continuation of high school, except the days of being able to mooch off my parents were definitely over.

There wasn't a class listed for playing cards, but had there been, my friend Howie and I would have gotten A's in hearts and kitty whist. Though hardly a mark of academic success, these games sharpened my math skills and increased my memory. To this day I still think I have a solid strategy for playing hearts.

THE FALL/WINTER SEMESTER gave way to the Winter/Spring semester. I was now bypassing "Oops" and going straight to the "Oh no" stage. My grades were settling into the D range. My GPA was a not-so-robust 1.5. Once more I needed to ace the final exams or there would be consequences. Not surprisingly, that didn't happen, so Newton Junior College asked me to leave. It may have been that I was bored with school or that I was better at cards than anything else. I just didn't fully understand what the consequences of my actions would mean in the long run. "Take a semester off, come back the following semester, and give it another try." No problem. There was still Aileen. Problematic to my relationship with Aileen was that she was Jewish and I was Catholic. To her orthodox parents that was unforgiveable. To this point they thought I was Jewish also. They associated my last name with the famous L.A. restaurant, Chasen's. This was my first introduction to prejudice. I should have known that Aileen had to succumb to their wishes once they found out I was not that Chasen. I had a full-time job with UPS. Money was rolling in, I didn't have to study, what could go wrong? Come the Winter Semester, everything was back to normal, or so I thought as I re-enrolled into Newton Junior College.

Around that time, I had a friend named Brian whose plan had been to join the Army. I don't recall what his reasoning was, but I do remember that his girlfriend was not wild about the idea. Occasionally I would get a letter from him from Vietnam. His letters should have scared the bejeezus out of me. Still it was his war not mine. Had I been paying more attention, I would have done everything in my power to prevent his path from becoming mine. Alas, hindsight is 20/20.

What was the big deal with Vietnam? Here's a bit of a history lesson to help make sense of what was happening 9,000 miles away. In 1954, French Indochina, also known as Vietnam, was divided by treaty into two parts. North Vietnam was under the influence of China and the Union of Soviet Socialist Republics (USSR), and South Vietnam had placed their trust in the United States. By 1964, 16,000 advisors had been sent to South Vietnam by Presidents Eisenhower and Kennedy. Up to then the country had been embroiled in civil war, but that was about to change.

In 1964, less than half of the population of the United States had even heard of Vietnam. They knew about communism and the "Big Red Scare" that was the USSR. Students my age had grown up with the Cold War and weekly drills of atomic bomb threats, but nothing about some small country in Southeast Asia. But on August 4, 1964, in the Gulf of Tonkin, the USS Maddox was attacked by three North Vietnam torpedo boats, which was deemed by the United States as an act of war. The next day, the U.S. retaliated, with Congress passing the Gulf of Tonkin Resolution, authorizing President Johnson to take whatever steps necessary in Southeast Asia. Neither Congress nor the American public then knew that a covert operation against North Vietnam known as Operation Plan 34-Alpha had begun in 1961 under the guidance of the CIA.

In 1964, the maritime portion involved three patrol boats operated with a South Vietnamese crew. Their mission was to launch coastal attacks against North Vietnam. Approval for these missions came directly from Admiral U.S. Grant Sharp. A revision of the original account shows that the USS Maddox fired three rounds to warn off the approaching North Vietnamese torpedo boats. This was never reported by the Johnson administration, which had insisted that North Vietnamese fired first. Four years later Secretary McNamara admitted to Congress that the USS Maddox had in fact been aware of the South Vietnamese attacks but not directly involved.

To prevent the so-called and dreaded "domino effect" (suggesting that if Vietnam fell under communist influence, other countries in Asia would follow like falling dominoes) and equipped with Congress' "whatever is necessary" authorization, the U.S. military put in motion Operation Thunder, a large-scale bombing of North Vietnam intended to bring the communist country to its knees. Military leaders projected that the operation would last only eight weeks, after which North Vietnam would be begging for a ceasefire. The plan failed. Some air bases in South Vietnam needed protection, and Marines landed in Da Nang, South Vietnam, on March 8, 1965. By January 1966, there were 180,000 troops on the ground in Vietnam, and a year later that number had grown to 390,000.

By January 1967, I began paying more attention to what was going on in Southeast Asia. Still, I thought I had no worries. After all, I had a plan, not to mention Aileen. Unfortunately, my plan wasn't the same as the draft board's plan. At that point, if a student made the mistake of breaking a college education's continual flow, it changed their draft status from "1S" (student deferral) to "1A" (draft eligible). That was a definite "Oh shit."

The writing was on the wall, I was just hoping it wasn't my wall. Early in the summer of 1967, as I was ripening towards the age of eighteen, I received a pre-draft notice in the mail. At this point, one-third of the U.S. soldiers in Vietnam were volunteers, and two-thirds were draftees. The draft had gone from 15,000 a month in the early stages of the war to 35,000 a month by that summer. Another friend, Doug Clark, whose girlfriend had just broken his heart, was dumb enough to join the Army just to spite her. Having nothing else to do that day, I went along for the ride to the recruiting station in Waltham, Massachusetts. Doug was swept off his feet by the promise of "Fun, Travel, and Adventure" (FTA), the new Army recruiting slogan. (New recruits ended up changing the FTA to "Fuck the Army.")

With Doug in his pocket, the recruiter turned to me, asking, "What about you, young man? Are you ready?"

I had been looking at brochures showing pretty pictures and listing all the exciting things someone could do if he were willing to give up six to eight years of his life. Ever since I was a child, I had wanted to be a doctor or a pilot. I enjoyed helping others as a child. I thought fixing their pain would be the altruistic way to go. Obviously, the doctor thing wasn't going to happen. College had shown me that in no uncertain terms. I was also fascinated with flight—perhaps it was the way pilots were revered in that era. I had no personal experience with flying but the thought of soaring above the landscape intrigued me. The brochures in the recruiter's office made flying look pretty cool.

"You mean I could be a helicopter pilot, even though I'm a college dropout?" I asked.

"Yes, sir," he said. "All you have to do is take a test, pass with a certain grade, and you could be part of the Army's new aviation."

I considered it for a moment, knowing the writing *was* on the wall, and decided, *why not?*

The next thing I knew, I was on my way to the Boston Army Base to take the test that would determine if I had what it took. I've never been very good at taking tests, as demonstrated by my failure to pass my finals in college, which would have kept me out of the Army in the first place! The call came a few days later. I had come really close but not quite close enough. The recruiter offered in consolation, "We have many other careers the Army can offer."

"No, that's okay," I said. "I'll just wait until I get drafted."

It was summer, so there was less time for Walter Cronkite and more time for other distractions. I just put Vietnam and the Army out of my head. That recruiter didn't forget about me, though. He must have been getting close to his quota and didn't want to lose me, so a month later he called and said, "There is a new test format coming out. You could retake that new version." The Army had realized that a different standard would bring in more people crazy enough to fly helicopters in Vietnam.

This time I decided to go to the library to see if studying would bring my score up. Wouldn't you know it, that studying thing worked! (Maybe I should have given it a try a little sooner.) The recruiter called, and this time he said, "Come in and sign on the dotted line." But it was the summer, life was good, and of course there was still Aileen. I told him, "Call me at the end of the summer, and then we can talk." I had no intention of being a part of his June quota.

The fateful day came at the end of the summer. I got my draft notice and also, coincidentally, a notice for the appointment for my flight entry physical. The recruiter informed the draft board that I had already signed up for a delayed-entry program, which meant I didn't have to go until the summer was over. I passed the physical and was told to report September 6 for swearing in, one day after my eighteenth birthday. I had no idea what to expect.

I'm not sure how I got to the Boston Army Base. I probably wanted to avoid a sad road trip farewell with my mom, but nonetheless I said goodbye to my parents, my family, and life as I knew it and took the subway into Boston. I reported as ordered, took the oath to God and Country, and was a member of the United States Army. There was one small hitch to the plan—I was told to go back home, as there was no transportation that day to where my basic training post would be.

Where would my basic training post be?

[3]

200 RAW RECRUITS

EVERYTHING I HAD heard suggested that new soldiers went to Fort Dix, New Jersey, for basic training, which was somewhat close to home. With Aileen at school in New Hampshire, there was a chance I might get to see her if I was in New Jersey. The Army had other ideas. I was headed to Fort Polk, Louisiana. Was that even in the continental United States? Somehow, it didn't faze me where I was going, who I would meet there, or what was going to happen. I was either utterly naïve or just stupid (I like to think naïve, I already had an idea about the stupid part from college).

I flew to New Orleans then caught a bus to Lake Charles, Louisiana, where there were a number of recruits already waiting. Almost everyone seemed scared and nervous, which wasn't surprising as there were sergeants yelling out orders of what to do and what not to do. It was chaos, close to midnight, and it had been a long day for all of us with no end in sight. A few were openly crying, others were fighting the urge to cry, and even those who weren't seemed shaken. I may have heard someone openly asking, "How do I get out of this nightmare?"

At this point I thought, *Thank God for Poland Spring Caddy Camp.* When I was eleven years old, my parents sent my brothers and me off to Poland Springs Caddy Camp in Maine. This was a financially effective way to send us to camp, as we paid our own room and board. The similarities between basic training and Poland Springs Caddy Camp were striking. New caddies being "attacked" by counselors wasn't all that different from being harassed by drill sergeants—being forced to eat a bar of soap if you were caught swearing, tying four or five cigarettes together as though they were one and having to smoke those down to the nub, the list could go on. Thank God for Bob Hatch and Chick Leahy, the two camp directors. In a way it prepared me for what was to come, though not quite on the same scale. After all, my first day of caddy camp was spent carrying someone's golf clubs for eighteen holes. The first day of basic training I was primed as a fighting machine.

The next morning, we all stood in a meeting hall, 200 of the Army's newest, waiting to hear what Army life was going to be like. The drill sergeant said, "Look to your left and look to your right. Those people are not going to come back from Vietnam, and that's where you are all going." My first thought was to look left and right and think, "Those poor bastards are not going to make it back alive." Later I realized that I was on somebody's left and somebody's right, and they were thinking I wasn't going to make it. Reality sunk in slowly.

Doug's best advice to get through basic training was, "Tell them you can drive a truck." Working for JG Willis years before, I did drive a sixteen-foot cab truck for a bit. When the drill sergeant asked, "Can anybody drive a truck?" I immediately raised my hand. From that moment on, I was the "deuce and a half" driver, no walking for me. The downside of being the permanent truck driver was that I missed out on some valuable training. For example, when it came to qualifying on the M-14, the drill sergeants were amazed that I couldn't hit anything. I tried to explain that it was my first time, but they didn't believe me. I won't bother mentioning drill and ceremonies and how badly I messed that up, let's just say the drill sergeants were amazed at my inability to turn around and face the other direction in the correct

Army way.

An important lesson was learned, however. One day at the range, one of the drill sergeants said, "I need a volunteer for a mission." (Doug never warned me about this part.) About twenty of us stepped to the front of the formation, and the drill instructor promptly said, "Okay get down and give me twenty push-ups." When finished, he warned, "Let that be a lesson to you: never volunteer."

I was feeling a bit foolish, but he proceeded to say, "Alright, lesson learned. But now I really do need a volunteer." He carried on about how important this was and even said there might be something in it for us if we were to volunteer. His sincerity won a half-dozen people over. He was quite convincing. In front of the formation, the dutiful soldiers were instructed to get down and give the drill sergeant thirty more push-ups. With that, he said, "These soldiers didn't learn the lesson! Failing to follow sound advice will get you killed."

It wasn't over though, because another drill sergeant came up about ten minutes later, saying, "I need a volunteer to do something for me." Most laughed, but he assured us that this was different, and he could either pick someone or just hope for a volunteer. After the embarrassed soldier who volunteered had finished his forty push-ups, the drill sergeant screamed in his face, "Never, ever volunteer! It will get you killed!" After some ninety push-ups, the soldier could barely lift his arms.

In addition to marksmanship, hand-to-hand combat, and drill and ceremonies, there was daily physical training, which culminated every few weeks in a test of our endurance and agility. There were five events: the run-dodge-jump, grenade throw, low crawl, monkey bars, and a mile-and-a-half run. I had always considered myself a fairly good athlete and assumed the Army would be no challenge. This proved true for the first four events, after which I usually had a score of 400 (one hundred percent). The drill sergeants loved recruits with a perfect score. It made them look good to the company commander. Consequently, for the final event I was always put at the head of the line. Back in 1967, we didn't have running shorts or sneakers—this run was in full uniform with combat boots. As a former baseball player, I could steal second or score from second to home on a single, but an inside-the-park home run was pushing my limit. I was a sprinter, not a long-distance runner. Thus, my drill sergeants stood in complete dismay, as I almost always finished last in the run. It took them ten weeks to realize I was never going to finish with a perfect score.

Basic training was otherwise uneventful, with the exception of the "Dear John" letter from Aileen. It wasn't unexpected, as I hadn't heard from her in quite a while. She offered the usual "You are better off without me" bit, which makes women feel better, but I felt like I should be able to decide what was good for me. I remember going off to an isolated spot rereading her letter, trying to fight the pain of rejection. I had no idea how long the hurt would last. I thought my life had ended. Slowly, the numbness wore away. It might have lasted weeks but the Army had other ideas to take my mind off the empty feeling I had.

THOSE WEEKS OF training were an acclimation of sorts and did provide one very important realization: that I had made an immediate connection with those around me. It's hard to explain if you've never been part of something similar—two hundred raw recruits in the same situation and faced with the same goal, challenges, and hardships. Close to forty recruits were straight from Mexico. They were given the chance at U.S. citizenship if they were willing to sacrifice their lives for six years. I often wondered how bad their lives had to be for them to take the chance of surviving the jungles of Vietnam. A number of others were drafted who had been holding out hope that the Army would never come to pass. There was a smaller number who were gung-ho, ready to fight for freedom and kill commies. All this time I thought it was the Viet Cong that we would be fighting. Perhaps they remember the drill sergeant's words putting them in the middle with some to their left and right.

In a very short period, it felt like we had known those around us for much longer than we had. We had become our own band of brothers. There was Don from New Jersey who wanted to be a medic. A whole lot of Italian in him made him seem a great deal bigger than his height of five-feet-six. Who could he possibly think he would be able to drag away from danger? There was Jon, who had actually finished college, which gave him an air of respectability. I figured that if he had finished college he was smarter than the rest of us. They all had dreams of what life would be like after the war—marriage, children, jobs, the American Dream interrupted by a few years of killing and dying.

I will probably repeat myself but we were in it together, us against them. The "them" were anybody who wanted to make our lives miserable at the very least or end our lives at the worst.

[4]

THE LONG RIDE TO

CHRISTMAS

THE END OF basic training coincided with Christmas. Broke, I realized I could either stay at Fort Polk and end up on KP or try to find my way back home. Ride-sharing seemed my only choice as I set out for the 1,700-mile trek home. In New Orleans I ran into some folks who were going to Rhode Island. I remember being excited thinking we were headed in the same direction and this would speed up my trip. The hitch was, these people had no affinity for the Army. Perhaps they knew what the Army represented whether it be involvement in a war with no reason or the danger of being drafted and taken away from their daily, carefree life. They refused to give me a ride under the pretense there wasn't enough room in their car for an extra person. "I'll even ride in the trunk!" I offered, but it was still a no. My only other possibility was going to the Tulane campus to try to hitch a ride, knowing there were bound to be college kids going home for the holidays. There had to be someone that was sympathetic to a poor soul trying to get home for the holidays, the Army be damned. I did get one, but only went as far as Montgomery, Alabama.

From Montgomery I lucked out with a series of rides until I found myself in Atlanta, Georgia. By then it was almost 2 a.m., very cold, and I had little chance of a ride that would put much distance between Atlanta and me. I set out hitchhiking, taking my Army coat off so that drivers might see my shiny buttons reflecting in the dark and not hit me as I stood in the middle of the road. I hoped they would see me and feel sorry for me. Car after car passed. I gave them the benefit of doubt that they just didn't see me until it was too late to pick me up, rather than assume that they didn't want to help a young soldier bound for Vietnam. Occasionally, someone would pick me up for just a few miles. I almost didn't care, as it was a chance to get warm for a minute or two. Around 4 a.m., God must have been watching and thought, "This kid is nuts, I'd better do something."

In "His" infinite wisdom, a lone driver stopped and surprised me with his offer: "I'm going to New York City, but I've been driving all day and night, and I just need someone to keep me awake."

I almost cried. "I'll sing. I'll dance. I'll do whatever it takes," I said. He explained that he was an FBI agent working on the disappearance of three civil rights workers in Mississippi. As interesting as his story was, it took me all of twenty minutes to fall asleep. So much for the singing and dancing to keep him awake! Somewhere in New Jersey I finally came to, apologizing profusely for not holding up my end of the bargain.

I was so excited to have made it this far. New York was only four hours from Boston. I had a $20 bill tucked into my sock and was torn between giving it to him or saving it for a Christmas gift for my parents. I decided to save it for a gift, however I had a bunch of change in my pocket, which I pulled out.

"Here," I said, "this will cover the tolls."

As I placed the loose change on the dashboard, most of it rolled down the heater vent. My savior of a driver just looked at me with a slight smile and said, "That's okay, kid."

A string of truck drivers picked me up as I made my way through Connecticut, dropping me off at locations that were good for finding my next ride. Finally, I made it all the way to Boston, where I was to meet up with old roommates. My last ride left me on Commonwealth Avenue, near Boston College, where I waited for almost an hour trying to catch one last ride to my friend's apartment, not more than two miles down the road. I was bound and determined not to simply take the "T." I had hitched my way across some 1,700 miles, and I wasn't going to quit now.

It was great to see my family and share some of my basic training stories. The $20 came in handy for some very small Christmas gifts for my parents. I also had a chance to see some of my old friends from Newton. At one party, I met a girl from LaSalle Junior College. Having been dumped by Aileen, I was very vulnerable, and fell head over heels for Linda. She may not have been as drop dead gorgeous as Aileen but she certainly came close and she was years ahead of any other women I had known if you know what I mean and I think you do! The torrid romance even found me visiting her in New York. This was the real deal, and in the back of my mind I thought, *Aileen who?*

After saying my goodbyes to Linda, I headed back to my parents' to say my final goodbyes there. I had promised Linda I would faithfully write, and she said she'd do the same.

[5]

From Snowbird to

WOC

HOME WAS GREAT while it lasted. All too soon I was on my way back to Fort Polk to finish the last two weeks of basic training. Then some forty of us were going on to flight school at Fort Wolters, Texas. Fort Wolters was just outside the little town of Minerals Wells and would be my life for the next six months.

We loaded onto a bus for the ride to Mineral Wells, all pretty pumped, as this was what we had signed up to do. Basic training was behind us, and we were going to get to fly helicopters. Fort Wolters had something of the same look as Fort Polk, but we quickly realized this was *not* basic training. Within seconds of the bus coming to a stop, a TAC (Training, Advising, and Counseling) officer jumped on board and screamed to the point of spitting that we were now his and would live to regret it. We were frozen in our seats as this demon bellowed orders at us. He finished with, "If any of you maggots has a change of heart, do it now! When you step off the bus, move over to the side, and save yourself the pain and aggravation."

As we slunk off the bus, three recruits made their way to the side as instructed so they would no longer have to put up with this abuse. Was this the beginning of the end? Would I die from some terrible torture in a little town somewhere west of Fort Worth, Texas?

For the next four to six weeks we would be known as "snowbirds." With the push for the new Army aviation, there were more bodies than helicopters, or flight instructors for that matter. We were put into a barracks with 150 other "wannabes" hoping to become pilots.

What we didn't know was that the next five weeks would make basic training look like a day at the beach. Every day we were up at 5 a.m. with endless hours of PT (physical training) to get us in shape. In the first week a dozen former "wannabes" dropped out, sincerely hoping there had to be a better Army out there. Each day was constant PT and classes of the military way. By lights out, we were all thoroughly exhausted, only to start anew at 5 a.m. the next day.

Adding to the upheaval in my life, Linda took exactly three weeks to write that there was no sense in carrying on the relationship that we had started. She figured there was no future for our relationship, and I was going to die anyway. This time it didn't take me by surprise. Love is grand while it lasts, but she was not part of "the plan," not that I actually had a plan. I was young and dumb and figured everything would take care of itself.

Meals at the mess hall were a new experience that we hadn't been exposed to at Fort Polk. We would stand at "parade rest" in line waiting to go in, exactly eighteen inches from the soldier in front of us, and then come to attention when it was time to move forward, before going back to "parade rest" again. All the while, four TAC officers would walk up and down the line, screaming questions at us. If we didn't have the answer, it meant push-ups. One recruit missed two questions and was ordered to go over to the nearest tree and explain (to the tree) why he wasn't worthy of becoming an Army helicopter pilot. I learned later that this was an organized tactic to weed out the undesirables. Those who failed now would surely never make it through flight school, let alone Vietnam. It worked, because by the time we had moved up to "the hill," as it was known, we were down to 115 able-bodied "wannabes" and we hadn't even gotten to the point of determining whether we had the skills to master flying.

My next "Oh shit" moment came at a Saturday morning inspection during snowbird transition. Throughout our time at Fort Wolters, we worked on a demerit/merit system, much like at West Point. We would get demerits for things we did wrong and merits for what we did right. If at the end of the week we had fewer than fifteen demerits, we got a pass, so in theory we thought we had a chance for a weekend off. In reality, we had better odds of winning the Powerball twice in the same week.

One beautiful but cold Saturday morning, I was the only recruit who had fewer than fifteen demerits. This fact must have slipped past the TAC officers. I was standing tall, waiting for the inspection, thinking I was looking good. I felt confident about my bunk area being perfect. I even had the guys pulling for me and double-checking my area. The major, who was our battalion commander, made his way to our barracks, with my bunk area as his first stop. He went over my entire area. Everything was as it should have been until he cast his eyes on my uniform.

"Soldier," he said, "your uniform is messy and a disgrace to the unit. That will be twenty-five demerits."

"Sir!" I said, "Candidate Chasson," which was the Army proper way of starting an answer or question. "That's impossible."

I was stunned. I had just gotten the uniform back from the cleaners the day before and I still had the receipt to show for it. My response didn't sit well with him. He proceeded to tell me I was wrong, and to make his point I was to write a 10,000-word essay on why my uniform was messy. To complicate matters, I was restricted to the barracks. He added that I would have to have the essay on his desk Monday morning or I would be gone by Monday afternoon.

The inspection for the barracks was completed, but I was still in a state of shock. Nobody could believe that he would make those demands, least of all me. A 10,000-word essay was incomprehensible. Other soldiers gathered around me to express their condolences. Some even said, "It was nice knowing you."

I FINALLY STARTED to write, and after maybe three pages of explaining that I had just gotten the uniform back from the cleaners, I was stymied. I had maybe a hundred words at best. How in the world was I supposed to come up with close to 10,000 more words on why my uniform was messy? I literally sat there for hours with nothing that would meet the major's requirements. Then an idea came to me. I would sneak down to the post library and gather all the material I could on the history of uniforms. Every branch of the service, even foreign countries and their uniforms. I would do the who, why, what, and where of uniforms. I would make stuff up if I had to, whatever was necessary to pass my test. The problem was, I was restricted to the barracks.

A group of us made a plan to get around this predicament. I would sneak down to the library, and if any TAC officers came looking for me, my fellow aviators would cover for me by saying I was in the bathroom and then send a runner to find me. In the library, I started copying, word for word, anything I could find on uniforms: why we wear them, how they are to be worn, what the different styles were, anything that would take up 10,000 words. I wrote until my hand became deformed from holding a pen. There was one instance where a TAC officer was looking for me, but the plan to alert me worked beautifully. I was in that library for eight hours on Saturday and was prepared to do the same on Sunday. My one mistake was taking a break from writing to go to church Sunday morning. One of the TAC officers came looking for me. He was all set to have me pack my bags for my direct violation of the battalion commander's orders when I explained I had only gone to church. He had a hard time trying to deny me the opportunity to ask God to help me write a 10,000-word essay.

After this near disaster, I was back at the library with runners in place to come get me. Finally I finished, having exhausted every iota of information and ending with the claim that my uniform was not dirty. I counted pages, took the average, and decided that I did indeed have 10,000 words of pure bullshit.

First thing Monday morning, I was in the commander's office to deliver my project. I was told to leave it and expect to hear from the major later in the day. My aviation career was in his hands, but I had done what he asked. Later that day, as I was summoned to his office. A TAC officer felt my pain and offered some advice as I was about to walk in.

"Do not argue with the old man," he said. "Just take it and keep your mouth shut."

In I walked. I snapped to attention, gave him my crispest salute, and said, "Sir, Candidate Chasson, reporting as ordered."

"Soldier," he said, "I have your essay here and it's 253 words short of 10,000." (*Oh shit* was about to turn into an *Oh fuck*.) "But I'm going to accept it with the hopes that you learned your lesson here."

I said I was sorry, adding that I really thought it was 10,000 words as asked.

He glared at me and said, "Go, now."

"Free to live another day," I muttered as I made my way out after another crisp salute. Afterward I had a celebration with everyone that had been pulling for me. I couldn't have done it without my fellow aviators. When my hand finally un-cramped from all the writing, I reflected on those who had helped me. There is a brotherhood that builds an incredible bond of togetherness. I wasn't sure if I would ever get my wings, but I knew without a doubt that I would never forget those who were there for me—future fellow aviators who were willing to risk themselves getting into trouble to protect one of their own. It didn't make a difference if they knew me or even liked me, it was us against them.

[6]

THE HILL

T HE HILL. That's what they called the area where we would eat, sleep, and breathe helicopter training. The first order of business was the assignment to a Warrant Officer Candidate (WOC) class. Ours was 68-515, 6th WOC, orange hats. Each WOC class had a different hat color to distinguish a member of that class from the other eight, as there was a new class every two weeks, approximately 115 students per class, month after month. (If I had stopped to do the math, I might have figured out Vietnam was going through an awful lot of helicopter pilots.)

As new students rotated in, they became the new "wannabes." Ours was the newest class on the hill and therefore subject to ridicule by other classes. That was okay, as we were just glad to be out of "snowbird" status. We were issued flight suits, helmets, flight gloves, and a TAC officer who would be a pain in our asses every chance he got. The word was that our TAC officer had been in Vietnam but had broken his leg in a car accident and had been sent home. Now, because of his failing as a helicopter pilot, he wanted to make our lives a living hell. At every opportunity he would jump in our faces to try and break us. He failed at this too, because as a group of WOCs, we became one.

It was us against him.

Each week, a new aviator was slotted to be the platoon leader or platoon sergeant. This rotation gave each of us the opportunity to lead and to take responsibility for the rest of the platoon of thirty candidates. My turn was coming, but I didn't realize under what circumstances it would happen.

The major who was commander of our class happened to love baseball and in lieu of baseball, he settled for a top-notch softball team. I had played on the baseball team when I was a student at Newton Junior College as a centerfielder. Here at the Hill, our team won a fair share of games against the other WOC classes, and the major was quite happy with that. However, on one particular Saturday after winning a close game, trouble struck.

We had inspection prior to the game, and I passed. After the game, though, I left my sneakers out while showering. Our beloved TAC officer came by my room and, spotting the sneakers without a proper home, gave me twenty-five demerits. In addition, I was to report to him right away. I was livid. I was playing on the major's team and taking a shower *after* Saturday morning inspection. What was I supposed to do? I did the regulatory three knocks on his door and entered, ready to do battle.

He sat there, smug and pompous, and told me he didn't care what team I was playing on, a violation of the code had occurred, and that was that. Standing at perfect attention through his speech, I was given the opportunity to reply, wherein I called him an asshole in no uncertain terms. His face turned bright red, incredulous that a candidate would speak to an officer in the United States Army that way. Then he said I could be faced with an "article fifteen" and kicked out of the program.

To make matters worse, another TAC officer was in the office at the time, listening to the whole conversation. He interrupted to try and calm the situation and, in my defense, said I had a good argument.

But—and with a very big "but"—he said he was a witness to the conversation, and although what I had done took some gonads, it was grounds for dismissal.

My short fuse had gotten the best of me. I walked out of the office where several of my fellow candidates overheard the loud conversation. We all knew I was in deep trouble. One fellow from Texas said, "Wayne, sometimes you eat the bear, and sometimes the bear eats you." From that moment on, my nickname was "the Bear."

I spoke to the major, begging for his counsel. He understood and said he would take it under advisement. My fate rested in his hands. Fortunately for me, my flying skills were pretty good. The major spoke to my flight instructor, who gave me a recommendation. I was saved and would continue in the program.

The insulted TAC officer (who didn't think I was warrant officer material) made me that week's platoon leader, saying he was going to watch me as never before. At the first mistake I would be out. I knew it was only a matter of time before he found a mistake. I remember holding a formation of the platoon outside his second-floor window, and I could see him watching me. I called the platoon to attention and had them take five steps backwards, so he lost his line of sight on the platoon and me. With that, I explained the situation to the platoon and said I needed their help. Once again, the rally cry was "us against him," and we would not give in. I finished the week without incident, living to fight another day, but I was ever-so-careful to not make a mistake or cross that TAC officer again.

Our days were split. The first half was filled with classes involving aerodynamics, weather, tactics, and anything they could think of involving flying, as well as mixing in classes on how to lead and be an officer in the United States Army. The other half of the day was devoted to actually flying. I lived for this part of the day.

Like all helicopters, the Fairchild-Hiller Helicopter (OH-23) that I was training on had a cyclic, a collective pitch lever, two pedals, and a throttle. Five controls that, if not in sync, could kill you. If I moved one of the five flight controls, I also had to move the other four controls at the same time to counteract Newton's Third Law of

Motion, which said, "For every action, there is an opposite and equal reaction." This had to be second nature to us, or we would never get our wings. The learning curve was seemingly an insurmountable task yet through it all it was exhilarating. At times I felt like this was what I was meant to do with my life, to fly. I never really gave a thought to what the future might have in store for me. I was living in that moment and I loved it.

A collective changes the pitch of the rotor blades all at the same time (collectively). Basically, this allows the craft to go up and down. The cyclic, in simplified terms, is the large vertical stick that you hold in your right hand. It controls the attitude of the rotor disc. If you imagine that the turning rotors are like a large plate, or disc, balanced on top of the rotor mast, moving the cyclic in any direction causes the rotor disc to tilt in the same direction. Because the main rotor gives a helicopter both lift and directional thrust, tilting the rotor disc vectors the rotor thrust and makes the helicopter move in the same direction the disc is tilted. Thanks to the main rotor's circular shape, the pilot can tilt it in any direction. And, as far as the rotor is concerned, it's just as happy going backwards or sideways relative to the helicopter's fuselage as it is going forwards.

Two pedals control the small tail rotor at the rear of the helicopter, which prevents the body, or fuselage, from spinning in the opposite direction of the rotors. Finally, the throttle gives additional power to the rotors, increasing speed.

Here's a short example of how all of this works together. Imagine we are both in a helicopter, sitting on the ground with the rotor blades spinning, waiting for our inputs to lift off. We slowly raise the collective in order to take off from the ground, so now the engine needs more power. Time to increase or "roll on" the throttle. As we become light on the skids of the helicopter, with the blades spinning in one direction, the body wants to turn in the opposite direction. We step on the left pedal to make the small tail rotor counteract this tendency as we rise into the air. To make matters more difficult, once we master this skill on takeoff, we must do the opposite to come back down: pull back on the cyclic to stop forward movement, reduce the collective to bring the helicopter back down, step on right pedal as the torque eases, and slowly release the pistol grip throttle so that we don't over-speed the engine. Make the incorrect movements and we could spin uncontrollably, which might lead to a crashed helicopter. This is multitasking in overload. There were times when I thought I would never master the complex coordination flying demanded.

1—*My first helicopter*

The culmination of our initial training came in the form of a solo flight. We went out to fly with our instructor as on any other day, but after a turn or two around the traffic pattern, the instructor pilot directed us to a spot at the side of the runway and said, "Okay, kid, take it around the pattern two times, and don't crash." After only ten or twelve hours of instruction, they set us loose to kill ourselves all by our lonesome. Looking back with the 6,000-plus flight hours I now have, I think he was absolutely out of his mind. I was still learning every day, and I didn't know what I was doing with only a dozen hours behind the cyclic. It shouldn't have come as a surprise because we knew that if we didn't solo by the fifteen-hour mark, they would conclude we weren't going to make it, and we would be asked to leave the aviation program, probably ending up as an infantryman in Vietnam. It was nerve-racking, to say the least. One by one, pilots were taking their solo rides. As the days passed, if we hadn't taken ours, we feared the end was in sight.

WHEN MY TURN came the fear that struck me was palpable as I sat in that OH-23, wondering if I could even make it around the traffic pattern, which was just a series of left-hand turns. I hovered out to the takeoff area, all the while looking for any incoming helicopter traffic. I didn't want to ruin their day or mine with a mid-air collision! Finally, I was ready for takeoff, and to my surprise, it went fairly well. Actually three-fourths of the traffic pattern was pretty exciting.

It wasn't until I turned on what we call "base to final" that I had the first "Oh shit" moment in my flying career. As I turned on to the final heading, the helicopter was sinking far faster than it should have. My first thought was that something had happened to the engine, and not only was I not going to advance my career, I might die in the process. I was getting lower and lower, no matter how much I pulled on the collective. Just then I realized I had forgotten one of the key components of aerial flight: I had reduced the throttle as I was descending, which was correct, but I needed to increase power to arrest my descent. Embarrassed, I twisted the throttle the exact amount, and immediately I was back in control and flying in for a good landing, if not a perfect one.

I had one more traffic pattern to complete. This time, my priority would be the throttle. I completed the second pattern and hovered over to my instructor, not sure if he knew how lucky I had been.

After completion of all flights that day, a bus took us back to our barracks. Once on board, the driver called out, "Anybody solo today?" A couple of the guys said, "Chasson did." The tradition after completing a successful solo was for the driver to take us to the local Holiday Inn, where all the mates on board would grab us and throw us into the swimming pool clothes, boots, and all. That was the second-best time I ever had in a swimming pool.

Of course, the instructors knew we were lucky to get around the traffic pattern without crashing, and they also knew it would be a while before we were trusted alone again. That was okay by me, as I wouldn't feel comfortable until I had more hours behind the cyclic. Training continued on without event. Unfortunately, there were individuals who couldn't get past the solo portion and were dismissed. I think we lost about ten hopefuls and were now down to 105 future aviators. We had reduced by almost thirty percent, and still had seven months to go before we could pin on our wings.

THIS STAGE OF flight training was much like basic training, in that we developed incredible bonds and friendships. There were seven of us who were pretty inseparable and always pulling for each other. Three were from California, one each from New Jersey, Chicago, Pittsburgh, and Massachusetts. We all had nicknames, either something from the past or that happened in flight training—Helmet, the Judge, Muff, Deacon, Snuff, Zee, and me, the Bear. John Biddar was aptly named the Deacon. John hailed from New Jersey and had successfully completed his bachelor's degree. The writing was on the wall so John had decided to try his hand at flying. As he was older than most of us we initially relied on his mature years for guidance hence the Deacon tag.

John did have one funny quirk that would be frowned upon in this era. John and I roomed together in a small area for studying and sleeping. Every morning when John would wake up before the alarm, he would reach down, feel around for his pack of Marlboro's that he had strategically placed the night before, all the while his eyes were closed. Through repetition he could light his Marlboro, take a deep drag, and with that he could open his eyes. I can only guess what would have happened if I had moved his pack of cigarettes to another location.

Brad, aka Helmet, hailed from the beaches of Los Angeles. Greg was from the LA area as well and his moniker came as a result of a rating system he devised for women. Crude and sexist by any standards it was something we joked about. Bruce was known as Muff. He was also from California, but from the high rent district of Los Altos. Not exactly sure why we called him Muff. Thinking back I might rename him the idea man. He always had a new way to do something or if there was a lack of something to do he had an idea for something.

Johnnie Auth was the Pittsburgh connection. We called him Snuff, I think because he was a touch on the short side. Snuff had a brother in Vietnam so there was a strong chance he would not initially have to go to Vietnam. That scenario just delayed the inevitable for him. The Army was not about to spend all their money for training only to have the newly appointed pilot spend his Army experience somewhere other than Vietnam.

Because of my near fatal incident with the Fort Wolters TAC officer I was the Bear. Sometimes you eat them, sometimes they eat you.

When our time at Fort Wolters came to an end, 105 Warrant Officer Candidates were transferred, either to Fort Rucker, Alabama, or Fort Hunter-Stewart, Georgia. Every one of the pilots in our band of brothers was heading for Fort Rucker, except me. I was on my way to Hunter-Stewart. This would break up the gang, and I would have to be alone again.

Then I heard that one "wannabe" had orders for Fort Rucker but wouldn't mind going to Hunter-Stewart. After talking to him and the TAC officer in charge of the assignments, I was cleared to make the switch, but was informed that I would be back on the original list if there was a problem, and, of course, there was a problem. The Army still had too many future pilots going to Fort Rucker and not enough going to Hunter-Stewart. Once more, I was headed for the state of Georgia with nobody willing to switch. On the day before the final assignments, I went to the same TAC officer, claiming that Jeremy Anderson was willing to switch, could I get back on the list for Rucker? The only problem with that was that I never talked to Jeremy Anderson about the switch.

I still wonder if he was pissed about the change in duty assignments. I may never know, but I felt relieved that our gang would stay together.

2—The original Band of Brothers

[7]

FLYING BLIND

W E HADN'T QUITE mastered the art of flying, but had successfully grasped the basics. Now, on to Fort Rucker, Alabama, where we would be schooled in instrument flying and the tactical maneuvers we would need in Vietnam. At Fort Rucker, we would be housed in an old World War II barracks, two to a bedroom with a small living area for studying and socializing. John "Deacon" Biddar and I had bonded pretty well, so we paired up. John was the elder statesman of the group. Not only was he the oldest, but he had a real college degree. He was from New Jersey with a great looking MGB and a girlfriend back home. John asked me to drive his MGB to Alabama while he reconnected with his sweetheart. Because it was Fourth of July weekend, I decided to take a detour to Panama City, Florida, before heading on to "Mother Rucker," picking up John along the way at the small local airport in Dothan, Alabama.

At this stage we were under the misconception that the Army had spent so much money on us that they couldn't afford to let us fail. That was only partially correct. During indoctrination at 6 a.m. the next morning, we were told that we would be treated like officers, there would not be anybody screaming at us, but if we were to mess up we would be told to leave, thus ending our aviation career.

The first helicopter we would fly was the OH-13, a Bell helicopter that would be our instrument bird for an eight-week period. Instrument flying allows flight in bad weather, without any visual reference to the ground. In other words, the pilot relies solely on an assortment of gauges to remain straight and level, as opposed to upside-down! Picture yourself in a swivel chair. Someone spins you around for a few minutes, then suddenly stops the chair and tells you to go walk a straight line. As you know, that is almost impossible. You can see where you want to go but getting your body to do that is another story.

The instruments in the helicopter tell whether the bird is going in a straight line or not. Our bodies and instincts tell us one thing, which we have an overwhelming desire to trust, but our minds have to rely on the instruments to override that natural drive and intuition. It can be confusing for anyone, especially a brand-new pilot.

To simulate flying in the clouds with no visual reference, we wore a device around our helmets to prevent us from seeing anything but the instruments in front of us. At first it was almost comical, even though we had an instructor pilot with us to correct our mistakes. This skill was no small feat to master, and I had a problem getting it down. After four weeks, we had a "check ride" to see how well we had mastered the challenge. Upon completion, the instructor (who we called the Hammer for all the pilots he failed) would draw either a happy face on the checklist or a frown. I got a frown. I asked him what I could do to improve, and he suggested that I sit in one of the helicopters on the ground and work on my "cross-check."

While watching the instruments, my head had to be on a swivel, only glancing at a single instrument for a second or two and then quickly cross-checking to another instrument. There were five instruments on board, and they all had to be in sync. I sat in a helicopter for what seemed like hours trying to get it right, as I was due for a re-check in two days and the consequence of failure was that

I would be held back for two weeks for additional training. I wouldn't necessarily be out of the program, but I would watch my band of brothers move on without me. The re-check came, and I passed, but there were several pilots who were held back for two weeks, and even then some of them couldn't master basic instruments and were removed from the program.

With instruments behind us, we moved on to tactical training in a UH-1 Huey, the same type of aircraft we would be flying in Vietnam. We were getting so close to our goal, and flying the Huey made it more real. Another benefit of passing instrument training was that we were considered to be the next group of aviators, and as such had a pass every weekend. This meant weekends in the summer in Panama City, Florida, which was loaded with more girls than I thought possible.

Every weekend we jumped into John's car, driving an hour or so to the beach. Because of our hair, or the lack of it, girls we approached knew they should stay away from us, put off by the fact we were in the Army. I think it was still too early in the war for that many people to have an aversion to the military, after all, we were in the Deep South. I think a better theory was they figured that if we were in the military, how long could we possibly be around for? They might have thought we looked at them as a "catch and release" kind of thing. If they could get past the hair, then we had a chance after telling them we were future helicopter pilots.

Another problem was that a gaggle of aviators approaching just one or two girls was a little intimidating, so we changed tactics and worked in pairs. Things improved, but there was still a problem: if we got lucky enough to talk to two girls, one might be a little more attractive than the other, which created a dilemma. The Judge thought of a solution, a formula for rating women. The rating system went like this: In its simplest form no girl was rated a hundred and no girl was rated below a seventy. A hundred was unrealistic and we were too proud for anything below a seventy. External factors that came into play consisted of length of abstinence, number of beers consumed, or in my case, just plain desperation. This sounds sexist today, but back in the 60s it seemed natural.

Each weekend excursion to Panama City we would break into pairs of two. One of us would be designated that week's "face man" and the other would be the "pig man." The idea was when you met two girls invariably one was a little more attractive than the other. The pre-assigned designations of "pig man" and "face man" meant there was no fighting over the attention of one girl over the other. And if there was a natural attraction between two people, as decided by the girls, all previous arrangements were off.

LIKE ALL SUMMER destinations, the crowds dropped off after Labor Day weekend, and we were relegated to entertaining ourselves in the area around Fort Rucker, which meant going to the one "wet" county in the area to drink. The Judge and Helmet introduced us to a drinking game called "Cardinal Puff." The rules were complicated, and under the influence of alcohol the series of tasks was almost harder than basic instrument flying. There were nights that we were downright shit-faced. Even back then we had a designated driver, as we were close to pinning on our wings and didn't want to jeopardize graduation day.

3—The crew in Panama City, Florida

During the week, tactics consumed our flying and classroom experience. After a period of time, we were let loose to act as two-man crews flying the Hueys—inexperienced pilots making their way around Southern Alabama, hoping not to get lost, let alone crash. At one point, two pilots ran into a problem with navigation on their way back to base. They tried to determine where they were, but finally called the tower and admitted they might be lost. The tower operator was very calm, asking the pilots if there were any landmarks that they saw that could help determine where they were.

"We can see this really big lake up ahead," they said.

"Turn around," the operator said. "That is the Gulf of Mexico and you've gone too far south." They never lived it down.

We also had classes on survival training to teach us the basics of survival when we got shot down. They never sugar-coated this, it was *when* we got shot down, not *if* we did. They taught us how to catch and kill a rabbit, skin it, and then cook it to eat, and I didn't even know they had rabbits in Vietnam. Part of our training also included the "Code of Conduct" a captured soldier must live by. We could give our name, rank, and serial number, but nothing else. Always try and look out for our fellow soldier during captivity, and never ever give in.

In one training scenario, we were instructed how to navigate on land from one area to another without being captured by a group of soldiers, who were to play the part of the Viet Cong. A group of us headed out, hoping to make it to the safe area before dark but were only into our "escape and evade" mode for thirty minutes before we were captured, tied up, and led off to a prisoner-of-war camp. Here we were introduced to some forms of torture. At that point I had nothing of importance to tell them, but I was ready to make things up if necessary.

Then there was the now-infamous "water-boarding." Picture the night as black as can be little or no moon. You have no idea where you are or what will happen next. Suddenly you are thrown to the ground and a smelly burlap bag is placed over your head. The acting prison guards start asking you questions while at the same time pouring a bucket of water onto your face. The feeling for me (and I would suspect for most everyone) was that I was drowning. You can't breathe, you keep hacking up water, and you try to answer their questions to get them to stop.

Another interesting experience was "pole torture." Our legs were spread greater than shoulder-width apart, we were placed at about half of our standing heights away from a telephone pole that was approximately two feet off the ground, and made to place our heads on the pole, supporting our entire body weight. After only a minute, it felt like someone was trying to drive the blunt end of a steel pipe through my brain. The pain was excruciating. Remembering that we were told to take care of our fellow soldiers and take charge of the situation, I stood up, grabbed Bruce and said, "This is against the Geneva Convention."

We were immediately dragged off to the enemy commander's office, thinking we were going to get shot. I thought anything was better than the water boarding and pole torture. Much to our relief, the enemy commander said we could go. He let the others go too, once they remembered lessons learned—that someone needs to take charge. Bruce and I left as fast as we could, knowing we were still far from the safe area and it was pitch black at this point. Five hours later we finally arrived.

The greatest lesson we learned was to avoid getting shot down at all costs.

GRADUATION DAY was closing in, and we were only days from our final task—flying from Dothan, Alabama to Fort Benning, Georgia, a cross-country flight culminating with an insertion into a landing zone (LZ) with ground troops stationed at Fort Benning. In the course of this exercise there was a very unfortunate accident. One of the instructor pilots, along with two soon-to-be Army aviators, was monitoring the flight when the helicopter they were in suffered a complete loss of its tail rotor. At low altitude, losing a tail rotor would take incredible luck to survive, especially over a wooded area; the instructor pilot and one of the student pilots were killed, while the other student survived but was severely injured.

Graduation day was a solemn event, with a fly-by of Hueys executing the "missing man formation" to signal the loss of two of our own. Much to my surprise, my parents came down for the graduation ceremony. Knowing it was a financial stretch for them made it especially meaningful to have them there, as a large number of graduates also had a significant friend or parent present for the occasion. My mom pinned my wings on, and it was a proud moment for all of us. On this day we officially became United States Army WO1s, Warrant Officer First Class. With our wings and rank, the Army now owned us for seven more years.

4—Me, my mom, John Biddar, and his mom

[8]

FLYING TIGER AIRLINES

BEFORE HEADING HOME from Fort Rucker, I learned that my parents no longer lived in Newton, having moved to Dennisport, Massachusetts, on Cape Cod. My father could do just about anything with his hands and had built a beautiful home on a saltwater lake. I didn't know anybody on Cape Cod, all of my friends from high school still lived in Newton. There wasn't much for me to do there, but I only had two weeks before heading off to Vietnam. The date was October 31, 1968, but we didn't celebrate Halloween. Instead, my mom wanted to have Christmas in October. We had a tree and everything. We got more than a few strange looks from the trick-or-treaters, who got their candy but were wished a "Merry Christmas" as well.

After several days on Cape Cod, I headed to Newton to see a few people. Aileen was on the short list, but that didn't work out. Everyone was convinced I was going to die, and they didn't want to be a part of that send-off. A high school classmate who had been a helicopter pilot had recently been killed in Vietnam, and they assumed I was next. Ellie

Wolf, Drew O'Malley, and Peter Cavallo were the only ones I connected with. They made things as comfortable and fun as possible, for which I was grateful.

Back at Fort Rucker, the "band of brothers" had arranged that we would all meet at Bruce Riddle's—aka Muff's house in Los Altos, California, as his parents had invited all of us to stay. We met just prior to our departure. Due to different deployment dates, we weren't there all at the same time, but it was great to be together with at least a few after all we had been through. Bruce's parents were so gracious to all of us. We had a wonderful last few days of freedom.

One-by-one the Band of Brothers left beautiful Los Altos, CA. We boarded a plane for Fort Lewis, Washington, where we would be leaving via "Flying Tiger Airlines" to Cam Ranh Bay, Vietnam. I was first out. Mike Bruce, the Chicago connection, was next, and then Bruce Riddle. Though we had hoped that we would all be in the same unit, or at least in the same area, we were spread out all over the country. We said our goodbyes, telling each other to be careful, to keep our heads down and our rotor blades turning.

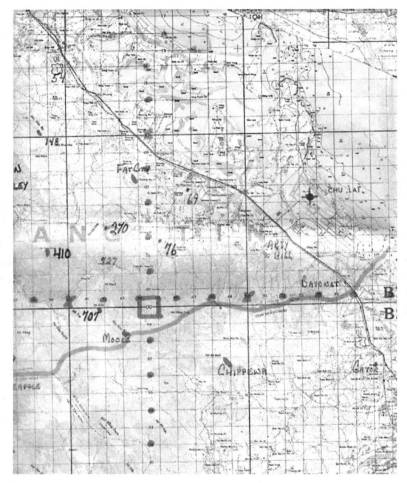

5—Map of the Chu Lai AO

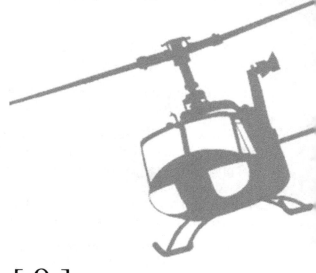

[9]

My Hooch

I ARRIVED IN Chu Lai on a C130 transport with about forty other soldiers. I think I was the only helicopter pilot in the group. Most of the herd was thinned, and I was told to sit tight as someone would be coming to get me. A specialist walked up and said, "Sir, you the new guy?" I guess my wings and brand-new uniform gave it away. He helped me with my gear, and we jumped into a Jeep and rode to our company area. The air was just as stifling as it had been on my arrival. I could smell the ocean and it made think of home and the taste of the salt air was similar to that of our family's excursions to Popponesset Beach on Cape Cod.

As we pulled in I had my first look at what my new living conditions would be like. We were situated at the very southern end of the division area, right next to the ammo dump, a little disconcerting. I reported to the battalion commander. In spite of my training in military etiquette, I was still afraid of making the wrong first impression. I knocked on his door, walked in, and said, "Sir, Warrant Officer First Class Chasson, reporting for duty."

When he returned my crisp salute, his first words were, "You are not warrant officer first class, just warrant officer."

Great first impression. He gave me the usual speech: "Pay attention. You are with a good bunch in the 176th Assault Helicopter Company. Try to get through the year in one piece." Maybe he had missed the briefing about how the one to the left and the one to right would not make it. I was about to tell him I was sitting in the middle and would be all right but thought better of it.

That was it. I was the brand new "peter pilot" in the 176th Assault Helicopter Company. For reference there are two pilots up front flying. One person on the controls and another that might be monitoring the radios or navigating to the next landing area. The senior or head pilot was the aircraft commander. He was responsible with everything the mission dictated. Conceivably, in the air he could tell a general that what he wanted to do was not happening. Now once on the ground the general could chew him a new asshole but in the air the aircraft commander was the final authority. The other pilot was affectionately known as the "peter pilot"—not enough time in country and definitely not enough hours flying the helicopter. His job was to watch, listen, and not screw things up. Our call sign was "Minuteman" for the slicks (general aviation units), and "Muskets" for the gunship platoon. The insignia was a replica of the Minuteman logo from the Revolutionary War.

Although there were other airports of entry, Cam Ranh Bay was the main entry point for new soldiers into Vietnam. My orders had me assigned to the 1st Aviation Brigade in Chu Lai, an area about sixty miles south of Da Nang. Not only would it be home to my aviation unit, it was home to the 196th Infantry Brigade, the 198th Infantry Brigade, and the 11th Infantry Brigade, as well as Marines and Seabees. This general area was known as Hi Corps or I Corps, and it stretched from the DMZ all the way to II Corps, Quinhon Bay, to the south. Not wide, geographically, but long.

The coastline of South Vietnam itself was approximately the same distance from New York City to Jacksonville, Florida. A small creek, just across from the battalion area, divided the 176th Company area.

A short 300 yards on the other side was the China Sea. It was a beachgoer's paradise. The sand was a brilliant white, and the water a crystal Caribbean blue. From the shoreline back for maybe seven miles it was sea level elevation. At that point the terrain went straight up as the mountains and terrain seemed to kiss the sky. From the air it was absolutely beautiful. The air was still hot in October and the humidity would take some getting used to. During the Monsoon season I swear you could stand ankle deep in mud and yet still have dry sand blowing in your face. Someday, we were sure, the Marriott chain or some other big hotel conglomerate would move in after the war, make it a resort, and get rich off of our sacrifices. In the big picture, what did it matter that there were sharks in the water? Only once in my eighteen months was I able to take advantage of the beach. That was partly due to the flight schedule and partly due to the threat of sharks.

The specialist took me to my quarters, which were referred to as my "hooch," where six aviators shared a plywood hut with a metal roof. My individual living area was about six feet by eight feet, which I did my best to make home for the next twelve months. There was also a "hooch maid" who kept our room clean and neat, making our beds every day, and washing our clothes down in the creek. Most hooch maids were probably thirty-five to forty years old, with very few teeth and unfortunately (or maybe fortunately) very unattractive. Their grasp of English was what they could pick up from us, which was just enough to communicate the basics.

Mosquito nets were our first line of defense for avoiding malaria, though they did give us two pills to take daily for the dreaded disease. One of the side effects was "the runs," which was a hard way to go while you were flying. I decided to take my chances with malaria and kept my mosquito net tucked in very tight at night. The furniture in my area consisted of an empty 2.75 rocket case for storage, an ammo can for trash, and a wooden stool. Any food had to be in the rocket case and shut tight or rats would walk away with it. That thought scared me more than the Viet Cong – I didn't want to wake up in the middle of the night to find rats fighting over what I thought was mine.

6—*Company patch with my call sign*

[10]

REALLY LEARNING TO

FLY

THE 176TH ASSAULT Helicopter Company had five platoons: three were strictly flying, one was maintenance, and one was administration. The first and second platoons were called "Slick" platoons, and their personnel were known by the call sign "Minutemen." The third platoon was the gunship platoon. They were known as the "Muskets" and their missions were typically for combat assaults, medevac recovery, or when the shit was hitting the fan.

The second platoon, which I was assigned to, had eight Huey helicopters. Slicks did anything and everything the Army could dream up for a helicopter. A mission might include combat assaults (CAs), resupply, medevac, or hauling Donut Dollies around. Donut Dollies were women volunteers who would occasionally go out to some of the safer firebases and try and cheer up the soldiers with tasty delights not often enjoyed by the troops, as well as games to play—anything to ease the thought of the jungle. I quickly learned that as a group of Donut Dollies would approach the aircraft, if you pulled just a slight amount of pitch in the collective the vortices would raise their skirts over their heads making for a welcome bit of visual relief. There were also recon, psyops, spraying Agent Orange missions—anything was possible with a Huey, which was fast and could take a pretty good licking. There were sixteen pilots, eight crew chiefs, and eight door gunners per platoon, all working in sync to do whatever it took to complete the mission.

On my first day I was paired with an "old timer," Ben Trevino. Ben wasn't old in years, but he had been in country for almost twelve months and was considered a "short timer"—someone who had less than thirty days left in his rotation before the freedom bird took him out of that hellhole. Ben was going to show me how they really flew in Vietnam, saying, "You have 150 hours of flying under your belt. I'm going to show you what they don't teach you in flight school."

We had a fairly light day, as it was expected that Ben would not be put in harm's way during those last two weeks if operations could help it. We flew by memory in our area of operations. Though we had maps, we learned the routes by flying them over and over again until it became second nature. And Ben was right, I had so much to learn if I was going to survive the next twelve months. Time and experience helped, but the learning curve was one day at a time, and I was impatient to learn as much as I could. Even in that dangerous environment, flying was still an exhilarating experience. From the moment of takeoff to cruising altitude all the horrors of war seemed to fade away if just for a moment or two. One minute you were dancing with the clouds and the next possibly descending into unknown dangers. (I still miss that every day.)

One part of that day's mission stood out: flying along an area that was on the unspoken line between U.S. Army territory and what was known to be NVA or Viet Cong territory. The gunner spotted an NVA flag flying from a lone pole. The gunner and crew chief were like two little kids hoping Dad would buy them a new toy. For a split second, Ben gave it a thought, but then he said, "It could be a trap." I was glad he was a "short timer" and thought the better of it. Even I had thought it was strange for the Viet Cong to announce, "Here we are."

Another "short timer" was Al Cerrullo, who later went on to be a relatively famous helicopter pilot by flying in a number of movies. I was a peter pilot walking around in a new uniform that stood out like the proverbial sore thumb. Al was getting ready to leave and asked me if I wanted any of his old uniforms. I gratefully accepted. Around then, the Army determined that the Americal Division, the largest division in Vietnam, which had its roots as the 23rd Infantry Division from World War II, should have its own aviation support.

The significance of this is slight, but it turned out to be ironic for me. In combat operations, we wore insignia on our left shoulder sleeves, which showed the combat unit we were part of. If someone had prior combat duty with a unit, they wore that combat insignia on the right shoulder, signifying that it was not their first dance. While our unit had been part of

7—Americal Patch

the 1st Aviation Brigade, we were now part of the Americal Division and wearing a patch on both shoulders. In Al Cerrullo's faded uniforms, I looked like a badass who had already done two tours. People steered clear, whispering, "That guy's done two tours already, he must be a whack job. Give him plenty of room."

THE WEEKS WENT by fairly quickly. We flew every day, climbing the learning curve along the way. William Joyner became a mentor, taking me under his wing and teaching me everything he could before rotating home. His call sign was Minuteman Two Three. I wondered if I would ever be able to be the pilot he was. He made it his responsibility to teach me everything he had learned. I was a baby learning to walk, so to speak, and I listened to everything he had to say. After a few days, he could see that I was tense, with a death-grip on the cyclic. Finally, one day he handed me a drinking straw and said, "Here, take this and put it between your first and third finger, with your middle finger resting on top of it." If the straw bent, it meant that I was gripping the cyclic too hard. There were more than a few bent straws, but things started to click eventually. Instead of trying to bully the Huey to do what I wanted, I began to ask her to dance with me. Like the lady she was, she didn't fight back, but followed my lead.

William Joyner also taught me the art of "contour flying," which was used only in certain situations. Any flying above 1,500 feet was usually out of small arms range, so we tried to stay at least that high whenever possible, but it wasn't always possible. Joyner said that too many guys, when dropping below 1,500 feet, would fly as fast and low as they could, just skimming the treetops, hoping that the enemy couldn't hit a target moving that fast. Joyner's philosophy was to fly five to ten feet above the trees and not quite at top speed. There were three advantages to this:

First, if you start taking fire from the enemy's automatic weapon, the tendency is to pull the weapon up, shooting above the target. If you were already skimming the trees, you had no place to go. Joyner's idea was to dive or turn, so that the bullets would fly over our heads.

Secondly, flying at maximum speed, a tree that was just a little taller and indistinguishable from others could bite us in the butt, cracking the windshield or playing havoc with the tail rotor.

Finally, as responsive as the Huey was, it could not fly at 124 knots and still turn on a dime; instead of being in control, the helicopter would just slide around a turn. When you needed the helicopter to do exactly what you wanted it was no time for her to not obey your command. If done right, it is almost artful and could definitely save your life.

Another trick was what I called the "100 feet, 1,000 feet" rule. You couldn't only be aware of what was immediately in front of us 100 feet out, you also had to know your next move or flight path 1,000 feet out so when you got there you were prepared. Flying along contour, you might suddenly realize you were in-between two valleys, leaving you high and dry. You needed to know what was coming so at the instant you hit that spot you could bank hard to avoid gunfire from both sides.

The mixed blessing of the Huey was the unmistakable sound it made. *Whop, whop, whop* was music to the good guys' ears. They could hear us coming from a very long distance. The bad news was that the Viet Cong knew we were coming as well. Even if they couldn't see us, all they had to do was point their weapons in the air and hope we flew over them. They had nothing to lose.

There was one almost-funny incident with Joyner that stands out. "Almost funny" because we could have been killed that day. We had begun to carry several kinds of grenades on board the helicopter: fragmentation grenades, white phosphorus grenades, and different colored smoke (CS) grenades. On that run Will included a CS grenade, thinking it would be a hoot to fly low over the village and drop it on the populace.

He was sitting in the left seat. To protect ourselves from incoming fire, we wore armor "chicken plates" to cover our chests, and there were also sliding chicken plates on the Aircraft Commander's left and the peter pilot's right. We were flying low, maybe twenty-five feet above the trees and village. He gave me the controls, saying, "Keep it steady, here it goes." Then he pulled the pin and threw the CS grenade out the window—at least he thought it was the window! Instead of making it all the way out, he mistook the sliding chicken plate for the window and let the grenade fall inside. Suddenly he yelled, "Oh shit! It's inside the helicopter."

The grenade went off, stuck between the door and the collective, and Will couldn't reach it. The cockpit immediately filled with gray CS smoke, making it impossible to see or breathe. Our eyes were burning beyond belief. I was trying to fly and Joyner was trying to get at the grenade. Somehow Will took the controls and managed to get the Huey on the ground. As the smoke finally cleared, I saw Joyner, the crew chief, the gunner, and a sergeant standing outside, coughing, gagging, and rubbing their eyes. I was still in the helicopter. We had landed on a rice dike, which put us at an angle pointing straight at the sky, making me think I was on my way to heaven. No such luck.

"Let's get the hell out of here," I yelled to them. The grenade burned a hole in the floor of the aircraft, which we tried to hide. The next day our company commander flew the same bird and wrote it up for having a "strong smell of CS." For days, anyone flying that particular bird flew with tears in their eyes.

I learned a lot from others too. For example, John Johnston taught me what a "high overhead approach" was. It started at 1,500 feet, which was supposed to be a safe altitude because that was the height that a round from an AK-47 could fly before gravity overcame it. (Of course, all bets were off if they were shooting something bigger, like a 51 caliber, or radar-controlled 57mm or 81mm rounds.) Part of the nature of this new "aviation war" was that we had to land at some point. To minimize exposure time, we came in at 1,500 feet, "nosed the Huey" over, and started a tight turn in a downward spiral toward the landing zone (LZ). To further help our cause, we came screaming out of the sky, at speeds of 2,500–3,000 feet per minute.

Most of the time we could make it to the ground in one piece. Unfortunately, after a while the enemy realized they didn't have much of a chance getting us on the way down, but they knew we had to come out of that LZ, and that there was no way we could come out as fast as we went in. They relied on the principle that "a Huey going down, must eventually go back up." We were sitting ducks, anticipating that we were likely to take fire until we could climb above 1,500 feet.

JOHN JOHNSTON and I flew in support of the Special Forces Group, working with "A" teams. "A" teams were units working with the local populace in hunting down "Charlie.*" For the most part, I was very lucky. We only had a few instances that truly scared me.

One of these occurred when we were flying from one "A" camp to another. We had to fly over a high plateau that then dropped off by 1,000 feet or so. Just as we crossed the edge of the plateau, the aircraft started climbing straight up, the cyclic moving uncontrollably into my stomach. John, who was busy with something else and didn't realize what was going on, said, "What are you doing?"

I replied, "I can't stop it." He jumped on the controls with me, and we both pushed the cyclic forward as hard as we could, but the ship kept climbing nose up. For a second, I thought we were going to roll over backward, which a helicopter can't recover from. Finally, and to our relief, the nose came forward, and we started to regain control. We still didn't know what had happened, but realized the hydraulics were gone, which was like trying to steer a car with no power steering. John radioed the Marines at An Khê, requesting that rescue crews stand by. We had to make a very shallow approach to execute a running landing to a skidding stop. As we flew in over the approach end of the runway, fire trucks sped alongside us, anticipating a crash. I didn't grasp the severity of the situation in the moment, but instead thought how cool it was that the fire trucks were side-by-side with us as we set the Huey down.

The next day, we were to pick up a photographer who was attached to one of the "A" team units. Unbeknownst to the ground unit when they gave the call for Minuteman 24 (John's call sign) to come in, an enemy squad was trailing them. On "short final" we started taking fire. It only took a split second for our thinking to shift from, "This can't

---

* American soldiers referred to the Viet Cong as VC or "Victor Charlie," the corresponding letters in the phonetic alphabet, often shortened to "Charlie."

be, this is supposed to be a safe area," to "We've got to get the hell out of here!"

I'm not sure what ever happened to the photographer, but he didn't get on our bird that day.

Following that mission, we completed a few more days of flying without further incidents. Then, as we were heading back to Chu Lai and Minuteman Manor, we spotted the Battleship New Jersey just off the coast of Da Nang, firing her big sixteen-inch guns. John decided we would fly out to the New Jersey and take a look. On the way, it was decided that the crew chief would be allowed the opportunity to fly the helicopter. This had two purposes: first, it was a way to thank the crew chief for his hard work; second, it was of benefit to the crew chief to know how to fly in the event the two pilots were incapacitated. This meant I sat in the crew chief's seat manning his free mount M-60 machine gun.

Normally, the M-60 was attached to a rigid mount to prevent accidentally shooting holes in the rotor blades in a tight turn, but that day it was "free mounted" – hanging from a bungee cord. We flew out to the New Jersey then headed back to Minuteman Manor. Along the way, I was cleared to fire the M-60 into the water. I started firing away, oblivious to everything around me. I stopped to let the barrel cool off and happened to look down at the permanent mount for the M-60. My foot was about two inches from where a bullet had gone through the mount.

"I'm done shooting," I said, offering no further explanation until we got back on the ground. We laughed, but I realized we would have had trouble explaining a hole in my foot when I was supposedly flying up front.

8—Members of the 2nd platoon; I am top row, far right

[11]

CLOSE TO THE VEST

I HAD BEEN in country for a few months, and up to this point loss of life hadn't yet touched our unit. We had our share of wounded pilots and crewmembers, but so far, no deaths. That changed when one of our aircraft was heading for Landing Zone Bowman. Bruce Macalister and his crew of Butler, Ford, and Bailey were hit by "51-cal" machine-gun fire, crashing with no survivors. I had been in flight school with Butler but didn't know him that well.

We were just two new guys hoping to survive Vietnam. Bruce was an aircraft commander with a little less than two months before he would return home. Secretly, we all hoped that if we made it through ten months the enemy had their chance and we could hope for some kind of amnesty. I was reminded how, during that basic training briefing when told who was not going to survive, in my mind it was always going to be the other guy. That day it was Merle Butler's day to be the other guy.

With that philosophy, the day-to-day stress and anxiety was easier to deal with. But war never gave a soldier a chance to mourn or say goodbye to fellow crewmembers. If bodies were recovered, they were taken to Graves Registration and prepared for the final flight home. After the aircraft crashed, we carried on with the daily routine. There was no wake, no funeral, just someone designated to clean their living area and send the personal property home. It was a morbid "here today, and no tomorrow." We were insulated through denial and immediate absence.

[12]

NOT LIKE IN THE

MOVIES

WHILE LEARNING THE art of flying, as I said we were considered "peter pilots." The lead pilot was the aircraft commander. The second pilot, known as a peter pilot (who sometimes was told to just sit and watch), was supposed to take in all that he could from the aircraft commander. His turn would come, after 200 to 300 hundred hours of flying time. Once we were proficient, or sooner if the shortage of pilots was desperate, we applied for aircraft commander status. Pilots were rotating home, and others were killed or wounded. Either way, a shortage made it necessary to promote a peter pilot to aircraft commander. I had flown on a number of combat assaults (CAs) and was getting close.

A CA is an insertion of troops into a landing zone (LZ), usually in Charlie's backyard. This meant that either they would be waiting for us or we could hope to take them by surprise. Regardless, we always expected to take fire in the LZ because once a formation of Huey's landed, we were sitting ducks. Prior to the insertion of troops, artillery from a nearby firebase, F4 Phantoms, or Naval gunfire would prep or "soften" the LZ in hopes of scaring Charlie enough to leave the area. With prepping complete, any number of slicks would tighten up their formation and prepare for the insertion. We had to fly as close as possible to the helicopter in front of us to allow the gunships to protect us on the way in.

My first and subsequent combat assaults were nerve-racking to say the least. Everything about the approach was slightly different. The temperature felt hotter, the air more suffocating, the noise on the radios could be deafening. Either on the controls as the aircraft commander or the peter pilot with nothing to do you expected ground fire. Why else would you be going in there if not to expect the enemy to be waiting for you. Although you wore a "chicken plate" for protection you really had no place to hide. You couldn't dodge a bullet, so you just sat there waiting for the impact of enemy bullets. You sat there waiting for someone in the flight to say, "We're taking fire." Some CAs went smoothly but there was always the anticipation of being the next target.

Depending on the size of the landing zone, the formation might include as many as eight-to-ten helicopters, but the norm was four-to-six. At a precisely timed moment, the escorting gunships would move ahead, firing their rockets and miniguns to further convince Charlie to leave. Sometimes it worked, and sometimes they just waited anyway.

The lead aircraft would usually take the heavy fire in an LZ. If the lead aircraft was shot down, those behind it would have to maneuver around the downed helicopter, knowing they might be next. Needless to say, it was nerve-racking on both approach and takeoff. If we were lucky enough to make it in without taking fire, we still had to get back out, and taking off could be a slow process. We had to take off as a formation so the gunships could provide cover for the entire flight.

PRIOR TO MY arrival to the 176th, there had been a peter pilot who, on his first insertion, took a bullet square in the helmet. It didn't kill him; in fact, the bullet pierced his helmet and traveled around his head, giving him a buzz haircut and a severe headache. That pilot was never hit again, but each time he flew on a CA, he feared it would only get worse. The anxiety alone almost killed him. That was one of the biggest problems, not knowing each day if it would be our last. We tried to suppress those thoughts and take it one day at a time because if we didn't we were doomed to live the next twelve months in constant fear. I was like many other pilots just past the age of twenty envious of those still at home enjoying the good life. I didn't want to die but had no recourse for what lay ahead. It was out of my hands as to the outcome of the next twelve months.

After a successful CA, we had to refuel back at the base. The formation would fly over Minuteman Manor, each trailing a different colored smoke, and break off one by one. It was a mini-airshow for the rest of the company and a morale booster for the flight crews. One by one we would bank hard to the left or right showing off our aviation skills. All the crew would take great delight in this aerial display. No matter how a combat assault went it was a welcome relief for just a few minutes to say, "We're back," and at least for this mission we were safe.

After we inserted a company or battalion of troops, they would spread out for their mission objective. We would then usually be assigned to support that particular unit or another that was inserted into the same area of operations (AO). It was a safe assumption that an AO had Viet Cong or NVA in sizeable numbers. If I went into company A's area and nothing happened, I still probably needed to go into company B's as well. If nothing was going on there, odds were, like playing Russian Roulette, that company C was going to be the one with the "bullet in the chamber."

I was building my hours each month, flying with different lead pilots and aircraft commanders, some from the first platoon, but mostly with those from the second platoon. Each time you could pick up something different from each of them. There was so much to learn. It wasn't as much a fear of doing something wrong as it was more of a chance to really hone my skills. I loved it. Every aspect of the flight was a thrill for me. It might have been the landscape we were flying over, and the quiet beauty at that altitude. It might have been the concept of me in control of a machine that not many my age would or could do. Even with all that might, there was a serenity to the flight, perhaps a calm before the impending storm.

Once I had an occasion to fly with Bruce Shaffer from the first platoon—not necessarily a risk taker, but he definitely went looking for any action he could find. We had come out of an LZ and were at maybe 500 feet or lower when the crew chief yelled, "We got dinks[*] in the open." Dinks meant the enemy. In this case there were two of them on the run. There was no mistaking these guys as Charlie, the black pajamas and AK-47s were a dead giveaway.

Bruce ordered the crew chief to open fire, and he promptly poured all the 7.62 ammunition he had from his M-60. Charlie must have been the luckiest guy in the world because the crew chief wasn't even close. After a few minutes, Shaffer yelled over the intercom to the gunner, a kid from West Virginia named Boyd Kettles who was the messiest, dirtiest individual you could imagine, even for conditions in Vietnam. There was nothing dirty about his weapon though. In all the times I flew with him, his guns never jammed. It was a thing of beauty to hear his M-60 firing away until the barrel got too hot. There was also nothing he couldn't hit. Shaffer rolled the aircraft around to Boyd's side, which was also my side, and yelled, "Don't let him get away."

_____

[*] A term used by American soldiers during the Vietnam War referring to all Vietnamese. For the sake of authenticity, it is used in this book with no disrespect intended.

Boyd fired a short burst, maybe six-to-ten rounds, and down Charlie went. We knew there was one more in the area, so we kept looking. We found him hiding in a small foxhole. Again, Boyd placed about ten rounds in the hole.

This was my first real lesson about the way people die. In the movies (prior to *Saving Private Ryan*), "death" looked like a person getting hit, falling over, and slowly closing his eyes. But this death was real: a body lying in a foxhole with no place to go, hit with multiple rounds from an M-60, will bounce up and down from the impact of the bullets.

That was the first person I ever saw die. I felt no joy, but no sadness either. I knew that some American soldier would have faced this man in combat sooner or later. It was his choice, his cause. I tried to forget it and move on, but sometimes I still see his body bouncing off the ground from the impact.

[13]

TIEN PHUOC NUMBA 10

WE DIDN'T PRONOUNCE it the way the local villagers did, the area known as *Tien Phuoc*. We called it "Tien Fuck." When our hooch maid would ask where we were going, if we replied, "Tien Fuck," she might say, "You no go to Tien Fuck. It bad, it numba ten." The number one was good, and the number ten was very bad.

One day, our mission there was an extraction of some sort, just a "klick" (kilometer) away from a firebase that had been attacked the night before. We landed at that firebase for a briefing to find the unit's exact location. As our crew was walking to the operations bunker, I happened to notice the Battalion Commander relieving himself along the barbwire. All of a sudden, he drew his .45 pistol and shot. There was a sapper, still alive and caught in the wire. Sapper teams were NVA or Viet Cong suicide squads that were extremely adept at sneaking through the barbwire at night, then wreaking havoc on unsuspecting ground troops. On more than one occasion, I heard of captured sappers who had shown their captors how they could sneak into the firebase without disturbing so much as a piece of wire or even the tin cans attached to the wire. We could barely see them even in broad daylight, so the chance of seeing them at night was remote. Needless to say, when the ground troops had searched the barbwire that morning, they had overlooked something. The Battalion Commander didn't miss a beat, but just went back to relieving himself.

We got our brief and boarded the aircraft. Just as the rotors hit full speed the firebase started taking incoming mortar rounds. I immediately started to shut the aircraft down as I watched the mortars being walked up the road toward our LZ. The gunner came up to my door and I yelled "Run!" I hadn't finished shutting the helicopter down yet, but I still beat the gunner to the bunker, that's how fast I ran. Afterward, we checked the bird (as we sometimes called Hueys). Luckily it had sustained only minor damage, so we decided to fly to the pickup point to make the extraction of the wounded soldier and called the unit for confirmation of their location. Normally, we would have had them "pop smoke" for their exact location, but in light of the mortar rounds, we knew Charlie was close, and we didn't want to make it easier for him.

We were approaching the ground unit on short final, low to the ground, when suddenly we started taking heavy fire and a few hits. The troops on the ground were yelling to get out of there, but we didn't need to be told twice. Taking hits to the aircraft meant it was done for the day, as we couldn't be totally sure that something wasn't about to go terribly wrong. We went back to the firebase to check the damage and declared it flyable, mostly because we didn't want to spend the night at this particular firebase, no matter what might happen on the way home. The thought of spending the night at a firebase was not my idea of a life experience I wanted or needed. The interaction with the troops on the ground was always brief—a stationary helicopter would be an enticing target to the Viet Cong. Even in those short moments on the LZ the soldiers had a faraway stare. Their eyes almost begged you to take them out of there.

AT THE END of the day I would always return to my base, Minuteman Manor. It didn't have the creature comforts of stateside but it was a thirty-inch cot with a metal roof over your head and a chance to take a real shower and brush your teeth. Having dodged mortars and sustained battle damage to the aircraft from AK-47s, we met our quota for that aircraft. We headed back to Minuteman Manor to get another ship so we could finish our support to that unit. After pre-flighting a new aircraft, we went back out to the firebase for resupply. The wounded soldier (our original mission) was not in critical condition (with just a sprained ankle), and the troops were laagering (camped) for the night.

Upon completion we started home down Highway 1 (the main road connecting North Vietnam to South Vietnam) which was deemed relatively safe, so we flew low-level. Flying down Highway 1 at a hundred feet or so gave you a totally different perspective of the countryside. Villages and huts sped by in a blur. Occasionally the village children would wave if they spotted us. They could hear us coming but weren't sure of which direction that might be from. Unbeknownst to us we happened to fly right over a firefight in full battle-mode. This was highly unusual as it was thought to be a safe route. The VC must have thought, *Why shoot at the ground troops when we've got an easy target coming right to us, and at low level to boot?* We had AK-47 rounds coming up through the center console, which separates the two flying positions by two feet. How the lieutenant and I avoided being hit will always be a mystery. We looked at each other and said, "Let's get home now and put this nightmare of a day behind us."

When we landed at Minuteman Manor, maintenance asked if we were going to wreck any other aircraft that day. Nope, that was it for us, but thanks for the generous offer.

[14]

MORE TIEN FUCK

THE NEXT DAY I was with Shaffer again from first platoon, going back into the Tien Fuck area so I knew what to expect. As we were flying, I told him what had happened the previous day—no worries, things like that don't happen two days in a row. The day was going along with the usual "ash and trash" runs, meaning we were to resupply the troops in the area with whatever was needed. We literally did everything in ash and trash: a medevac, a photo recon, almost any conceivable use of Army aviation.

Suddenly, over the radio came the words we never wanted to hear: "We're going down." One of our sister ships either had an engine failure or was being shot down but was able to call for help. We were in the area and responded that we were on our way. A gunship team heard the call and was on the way as well. At this point we didn't know if it was a shoot-down or an engine problem, only that we had to get these guys out, especially given the area of operations. We spotted smoke in the distance and figured that was the best place to start looking. The downed crew had made it to an LZ that was big enough for two helicopters. Normally, the A/C (aircraft commander) took over in this type of situation and I, as the peter pilot, would follow him on the controls in case he got hit. Just as we were making our approach, the gunship team arrived to give us as much fire protection as possible as we landed. A couple of Marine A-4 jets had also heard the call and communicated that they were on station, and to holler if we got into the shit. After what seemed like hours on the ground, the downed crew finally made their way to our aircraft.

"We're coming out, cover us," Bruce calmly called out to the gunships. The gunships rolled in and started laying down whatever ordnance they had left. Bruce pulled all the pitch the ship had, and we climbed as fast as the helicopter was capable of. We got to about 500 feet and everybody from the downed crew was slapping us on the back and hugging. We were all relieved that it worked out without taking any additional fire.

The Marine jets decided to roll in and drop whatever bombs they had on board for additional cover. Now, a jet flying at 400mph isn't the most agile of aircraft. I looked up and saw the A-4 drop a load of 250-pound bombs then pull up out of his break and I realized he couldn't maneuver quickly enough to avoid slamming into us in a mid-air collision. Schaffer was focused on the celebration in the back so I grabbed the controls and yanked the Huey to the right. We almost lost the downed crew out the cargo door, and Schaffer was about to say something like, "What the fuck" when he saw the A-4 pass maybe a hundred feet from us. I don't know whose eyeballs were bigger, Schaffer's or the marine flying the A-4, but I can tell you the pilot of the A-4 had blue eyes.

Celebration time was over. It was time to get back to the Manor in one piece. We had just made a pretty good rescue, only to see it almost end in catastrophe.

WAYNE CHASSON

PART 2:

ON THE CONTROLS

[15]

NO MORE TIEN FUCK . .

. PLEASE

THE NEXT DAY I was assigned as peter pilot to fly with Barry Lamkin, another first platoon aircraft commander. He was a relatively new A/C, and they liked to match a senior peter pilot with a newer A/C. As it turned out Barry was from Plymouth, Massachusetts, just over the bridge from Cape Cod. He had a big bushy haircut that made you wonder how he was able to get his helmet on. Our mission for that day was split into two parts. First was a milk run of sorts, in a relatively safe area of operations. The second half was to support troops in the Tien Fuck area. Naturally I was thinking, *The third time is the charm*, hoping that this was not going to be my "oh fuck" day.

As we shut down at midday for chow, I decided that the crew should know what the area was really like and the precautions we should make. The crew chief and gunner were hanging on my every word, but Barry didn't want anything to do with the conversation, he didn't want any negative vibes and thought it was a little extreme to talk about it.

"I've been in this area for the last three days," I said, "and this is what we need to be prepared for *when* we get shot down, not *if* we get shot down."

Our mission was to get some badly needed resupplies into this tiny LZ and carry out whatever wounded we could. We would have gunship coverage going in and coming out, which made me feel a little better. Barry had a great idea. We would make a descent into a fake LZ, where troops in this location would pop smoke, hopefully tricking the VC into thinking that was where we were going. Then, with guidance from the gunships, we would fly contour to the real position of the troops, make our drop, and pick back up as fast as possible. We didn't need to linger because the ground troops had already told us that the enemy were all around them.

We started into the fake LZ with Barry on the controls. At that point, the peter pilot's job was to just follow along on the controls in case something bad happened. The Huey was very responsive, and the tail-rotor pedals highly sensitive to inputs, so I followed the A/C movements on the collective and the cyclic but kept my feet flat on the floor of the aircraft. As we were descending, I was scared shitless, saying every prayer I could think of, asking God to get me through this—*I'll stop swearing, I'll stop smoking, I'll do whatever, just please God, get me through this.* It wasn't a matter of *will* we take fire, it was a question of *how much* and *will I survive?* That was a different feeling than those on all the previous combat assaults I had been on. The wondering and anticipation were not issues, it was just a matter of *when.* My mind was racing a thousand miles an hour to nowhere, just a blur. Barry's concentration was on flying. Training took over. The job he had to perform consumed him. I had nothing to do except sit there and wait, which made room for my fear.

We reached the fake LZ where the gunships started giving us clock directions to fly and the distance to go. "You have 3,000 feet to go…

2,000 feet to go… 1,000 feet to go." The next thing I heard over the radio was, "You've gone too far." Barry yanked the cyclic back into our chests, bottoming the collective so that the helicopter basically stood on its tail, the rotor blades creating a huge force forward rather than downward. Good news-bad news: the NVA had been hiding in spider holes inside the unit's perimeter, and as we came to a stop with our tail pointing to the ground, the NVA opened fire (the bad news). The good news was that the bottom of our seats were bullet proof, and we were wearing chicken plate, which was designed to stop a round from a distance of maybe 75–100 feet and out. I had been told not to wear it tight to my chest. It's difficult to describe the sound of all the gunfire: the NVA's AK-47s, the Army's M-16s, and the gunships trying to cover us with M-60 machine guns, rockets, and mini-guns. It was a cacophony of bullets. The automatic weapons fire from both the Viet Cong and American soldiers seem to fill the air with a solid lead wall. The aircraft started to shake with the impact of AK-47 rounds. I was yelling to the two hapless soldiers in the back to kick out the ammo. No need to tell our crew chief and gunner as they were adding to the noise with their own M-60 machine guns.

At that moment Barry got hit through the foot, the bullet traveling up into his leg. He flailed back, and suddenly I was on the controls. Just like that, I had a job to do. I was no longer scared shitless—I had something to keep me occupied and not thinking about how much fire we were taking. The next thing I knew bullets were coming through the cockpit dashboard and instruments exploded in front of me. We were now coming out of our tail-upright position into a more level position and with that, I got hit right in the chest. It felt like someone had taken a hammer to my chest, knocking all the air out of my lungs. Not keeping my chicken plate tight to my body allowed the impact to be absorbed and deflected as the plate collapsed into my chest.

I was okay, still flying, with something to concentrate on. I focused on getting the ammo resupply out to the troops and the wounded onboard. With all the firing going on the ground troops were going to need the ammo. The two soldiers we had taken along to be replacements (lucky them!) were kicking the ammo out as fast as they could. I felt a hot sting in my hand and leg but was too consumed to notice with all that was going on. The gunships were yelling over the radio for me to get the hell out of there—they were just about out of ammo. Barry was hit and I was trying to get low enough to have the ground troops throw the wounded on board, but the gunships were insistent. I turned the aircraft to the right and headed for a Special Forces camp about two klicks away. The crew chief came forward from his gun position and was pulling Barry out of his seat. He laid Barry next to the extremely lucky replacement soldiers, for them to try to stop the bleeding. The crew chief started to climb into Barry's now-vacant seat. His intention was to take over the controls. My first thought was, *No way I am giving up these controls. As long as I have something to do I won't be able to think about what just happened, or realize my hand and leg still have this burning sensation.* The crew chief thought I was hit as well because the instrument panel and windshield were shot up pretty good, and I was not responding to anyone.

I thought that as bad as Barry was I should try to get him to the 27th Med Hospital. I was trying to climb to altitude and the gunships were still covering us. They were calling me to find out the condition of the crew and helicopter. The crew chief finally determined that I was capable of flying, and the reason for no communication was that the cord from my helmet had been shot in half. He climbed into Barry's seat, and I leaned toward him to put on Barry's helmet and talk to the gunships. I told them Barry was hit pretty badly but I thought I could make the hospital. The Huey, with all its battle damage, was still flying but was cocked off to about a thirty-degree angle sideways. I thought I had some kind of tail-rotor malfunction.

You'll remember that my initial job in the operation was to have my hands close to the controls in case something like this happened, yet my feet were to stay away from the sensitive pedals. So here I was, flying off at a thirty-degree angle, leaning over to the other side of the cockpit, trying to communicate with the gunships, and trying to get to the hospital. At that moment, I looked down at my feet and sure enough, they were still flat on the floor. I had never, in all the excitement, placed my feet on the pedals. I looked around to see if anybody noticed, then put my feet on the pedals, and that wounded duck turned straight into the wind as though nothing was wrong.

Naturally I was embarrassed, but relieved that maybe we would make it to the hospital intact.

THE GUNSHIPS CALLED ahead to alert the hospital, and I landed without further incident. The hospital personnel were ready with a gurney to take Barry inside. Once they were clear of the helicopter, I lifted the Huey to make the flight back to Minuteman Manor. I did a very shallow approach in case anything went wrong during the landing. The gunships had already landed, so word had spread pretty quickly about what had happened, and people came running up to us with handshakes and "attaboys."

The Huey had taken quite a beating but kept on ticking. Those from the company that came out were pouring over the aircraft counting holes, two of which came through Barry's side of the windshield. Someone took his helmet and placed it on the area between two bullet holes, concluding that the bullets couldn't have missed his head by more than a couple of inches.

While all this was going on, the battalion commander himself came up to the ship. He looked around at the aircraft, looked at me, then back to the aircraft.

"Chasson," he said, "from what I hear, you did a good job getting in and out of there and getting Barry to the hospital, but *what the hell were you thinking* when you decided to leave the safety of the ground at the hospital and fly this bird back here? You should have stayed right at the hospital and waited for another bird to come get you. At any time that aircraft could have quit on you. Are you crazy?"

Well, he was absolutely right. I wasn't thinking. I was still in shock and had just reacted to the situation.

"Sorry, sir," I said. "It will never happen again, at least I hope not."

I walked back to my hooch, still in kind of an out-of-body experience and not fully realizing what had happened. It might have been Tom Mellon who came over and said, "Do you know you're bleeding?"

I realized I had taken some shrapnel to my hand and leg when my cockpit door was riddled with bullets. Off to the flight surgeon for a little care, and I was as good as new in a couple of days. Later that night the gunner and crew chief thanked me, saying I had been right about that area. I never saw Barry Lamkin in country again. I also never shared my "feet stuck to the floor of the cockpit" story with any of the Minutemen, though I did tell my buddies Dwight and Geoff many years later when we were in the National Guard. (Twelve years later things like that can seem a whole lot funnier and not quite so embarrassing.)

That night was one of the few times I went to the O club for a beer. We were always flying, and I didn't trust my skills when flying with a hangover. After a few drinks, everybody had a "there I was" story, and they all ran together. It was just a time to relax and forget about the war, or at least about what tomorrow's mission might bring.

[16]

MINUTEMAN TWO-

THREE

WELL, AFTER THE incident with Barry (who was being shipped home) the major and my platoon leader must have decided, "We need to replace Barry, and Chasson will be it." That or they felt sorry for me about the previous three days and thought, "What the hell, he hasn't died yet." So, I was a brand-new aircraft commander in the second platoon. William Joyner had rotated home, and I was to carry on the legacy and be known as Minuteman Two-Three. My first day, operations paired me up with Fast Eddy Covill. We had come into the country about the same time, I was maybe a week or two ahead of him. Ed ran about six feet tall with a wiry moustache that any twenty-one-year-old might have trouble growing. We called him Fast Eddy for the opposite reason you would think—except for being scrambled for an emergency mission he moved relatively slow. One thing you could count on with Ed was the long unfiltered Pall Malls he used to smoke. Kind of reminded me of home as my mom smoked the same brand. The philosophy of matching a new A/C with a senior peter pilot meant Eddy and I were destined to be together.

We were assigned to resupply a unit that hadn't had supplies in a few days. We headed out into weather that was borderline for the area, the hill they were on was enshrouded in fog. Aircraft commanders sat in the left seat of the helicopter. Vision was less restricted by the forward panel, so approaches often gave us a better view than from the right seat. The instruments for flying were better from the right seat but flying into zero-visibility was never a good thing, so we tried to avoid it at all costs.

As we got closer, the ground unit tried to give us directions, as popping smoke wasn't going to help with all the fog. We started our descent and quickly went IMC, which is when you no longer have visual reference to the ground and must rely on instruments to keep straight and level. Although I had been flying, Fast Eddy took over the controls since the instruments were better on his side. There were more instruments specific to instrument flying on the right side of the aircraft. The left side had less of a panel of instruments but it also had a much better visual view to the area below and outside the helicopter. One situation that could cause an "oh shit" moment was when someone couldn't make the adjustment from visual reference to instruments, and Ed was having a bit of a problem, so I took the controls back.

Trying to fly off the instruments on the right side is tough enough, but trying to fly instruments on the left side was an incredible challenge. I kept trying to look over at the instruments on the right side to give me a better chance of staying upright. The only problem was that when I looked at the instruments on the right side I was looking at them at an angle. Subsequently, although I thought I was flying straight and level, I was actually in a very slow albeit coordinated right turn. At this rate I would be flying in a circle in no time. We kept descending, hoping to see the ground. We knew we were in the mountains, we just didn't know where the mountains were in relation to us.

All of a sudden the crew chief yelled, "I've got the ground but don't come left, it's a mountain."

The gunner then said, "Don't come right, I've got a mountain as well."

Oh shit, we were in a valley, and lucky I didn't crash into either side. I made a quick decision, with Ed's approval, to keep descending to the valley floor and then point the aircraft due east, towards the ocean. (The ocean was my friend, as I figured the enemy couldn't be out there.) We contoured, low level, all the way to where we could climb to a safe altitude. Once above 1,500 feet we called the ground unit again and said the weather was too bad, we didn't think we could make it.

"No problem," they said, "no one else has been able to make it either."

I learned from that experience, just like I tried to learn from all my other near misses. Unless someone on the ground was dying or in really dire straits, the loss of four lives was not worth the mission. After three days working the Tien Fuck area, Fast Eddy Covill dubbed me "Magnet Ass." Most every unit had one. A magnet ass was someone who seemed to attract lead—as in *lead* from small-arms fire. The next day, Ed made aircraft commander. I guess the major and platoon leader figured having Ed and I together was pushing the envelope.

[17]

WALL OF SHAME

OUR HOOCH WAS divided into six-to-eight-man cubicles. Each man had four plywood walls, with a beaded screen or something similar for a door. On the outside of each room the plywood made a hallway with one exit at each end. People might post a sign or a message on the walls of the hallway, as well as pictures, clippings, and of course the Playmates of the Month (the monthly centerfold pictures).

One particular night, I was fast asleep on my bunk, facing my door. I woke up in the middle of the night. I was sure I saw a Viet Cong who had snuck into our company area and was now in my hooch. I lay perfectly still, watching him move back and forth ever so slowly. I didn't think he had seen me. He would move a little and then stop. I couldn't tell what his plan was, but I was a nervous wreck waiting to have my throat slit. After what seemed like hours—me watching him, him watching me—I slowly reached down to pull up my mosquito net so I could make the first move. My weapon was too far away, so I planned to surprise him, maybe scare him into running off. With one motion and a bloodthirsty scream, I leapt from the bed towards Charlie. What I grabbed was Miss December, swaying ever so gently back and forth because she had lost a tack. Of course, the blood-curdling scream woke my hooch mates, as well as the guys next door. I proceeded to rip every Playmate from the wall while my fellow pilots wondered what had just happened. After explaining how I thought they had all been killed in their sleep by a VC sapper, they had quite a laugh. I didn't get much sleep that night but there were no more pictures on the wall from that point on, so I guess I did my part in reducing the exploitation of women.

As I mentioned earlier, we would decorate our rooms with whatever materials we could find. In most cases, it was empty ammo cases or rocket cases. We were advised to keep anything edible locked up or at least shut very securely in these cases. Johnny Johnston forgot that rule one night, and as he was sleeping he heard a rustling above his head where his art deco rocket case was. As he turned on a light, a rat the size of a small cat decided feeding time was over and the quickest way out of the hooch was across Johnny's chest toward the door. John said the rat hesitated for a split-second and gave him a look like, "Is that all you got?" My blood-curdling scream from the attack of Miss December was matched by John's as the rat beat a hasty retreat out the door. Naturally, the rest of us didn't just wake saying, "Oh, is something going on? Let me go see." No, we came out with guns drawn, ready to repel an invasion. We had a good laugh over that, but poor John was a wreck for the rest of the night.

If we ever had a morning constitutional, we were lucky. Often we were taking off at the break of dawn, so that wasn't always a luxury one could afford. Usually we had to relieve ourselves at night, which presented two problems because our outhouse was very close to the noncommissioned officer's club. Imagine walking to the outhouse, a plywood structure maybe four feet by six feet. The procedure for entering the "john" was to bang loudly on the door, wait a few seconds, then open the door and stand back to allow any rats to leave before you entered. If you were lucky, all would leave and your only trouble, sitting in the dark hoping the rats would stay away, was to listen to awful old-time country/western music blaring from the NCO club. Now I love today's country western music but this was real old hard-to-listen-to music. The smell took on an aroma of its own and the constant dampness made for very soggy toilet paper. It was a miserable torture, especially if you were constipated. Once outside you needn't bother to leave the door open for the rats that always found their way back in.

[18]

RED CROSS-ORDERED

MAIL

MAIL TO AND from the States was normally a two-to-three-week process. Send something out, and if the reply was immediate, you would get a response in two weeks, best-case scenario. In the beginning, I was not the best correspondent to my parents. Every time a helicopter was shot down, my parents would worry that it was my helicopter, even though the country stretched almost as long as the East Coast. To ease my mom's fears, when I did finally respond I told her not to worry, I was going to be working in the maintenance section of the 176th. The war for me would just be repairing helicopters and test flights. Of course, it was a big lie, but I didn't want them to worry all the time. That worked for a while, but I never was the best letter writer. At one point, my mom even sent postcards that had the address already made out on the front. On the back there were four phrases written out, and all I had to do was check a box and send it back. What could be easier than that? The phrases were something like, "I'm fine," "I'm fine and will write soon," "I miss you and will write soon," and, as a joke, "I'm dead and will not be writing back." She was quite the jokester.

After a fairly long period of my not writing back, they got quite worried. My sister had an old boyfriend who worked in the White House for Nixon as appointment secretary, and she made some phone calls. One day I was walking past company headquarters and the company commander, Major Hite, saw me and banged on the window saying, "Chasson, get in here." I immediately turned around, not sure what he could want. I didn't even think he knew my name. I went in to the orderly room and asked the first sergeant what the commander wanted with me. He said, "I have no clue, but it can't be good." I knocked, went in, and gave him a crisp salute. That was twice now that I had to salute in Vietnam.

"Chasson," he asked, "when was the last time you wrote home?"

"Oh, I don't know, sir, maybe a week or so ago."

"No, it's been almost two months. Go write a letter home."

Oops. I guess it had been a while, but how did he know?

I went back to my hooch and wrote a nice letter to my parents, then went back to what I was doing. I had been on my way past the company headquarters to check on my aircraft for the next day. As I was walking past the commander's office a second time, he saw me and again banged on the window. "Chasson, get in here."

I hustled inside and again asked the first sergeant what was up. He said, "I don't know, but it can't be good."

Into his office I went, and with my third crisp salute in Vietnam, I asked, "What can I do for you, sir?"

He squinted his eyes and said, "Where's the letter?"

"Back in my room, sir."

"Go get it and mail it now. The postage is free."

"Yes, sir," I replied, and I mailed the letter home right then and there.

The next day I was once more walking by the major's office. He saw me again, banged on the window, and said, "Chasson, get in here."

Man, I thought to myself, *what is going on?* Once more I asked the first sergeant, "What's up?"

Again, he replied, "I don't know, but it can't be good." (He wasn't a very helpful first sergeant.)

I'm counting now, because in a war zone we didn't usually salute, as the enemy then would know who the officers were. I was up to four salutes after I entered his office.

"Chasson, when was the last time you wrote home?"

I thought he was joking, and said, "Yesterday, sir. You saw me."

"You mean you didn't write home today?"

Again, I thought he was joking, so I said, "Sir, I have another six weeks or so before the next one."

He didn't think that was funny. He got real serious and said, "Chasson, I have more important things to do than make sure you're writing home. If the Red Cross gets in touch with me again, I am going to make your life a living hell."

"Yes, sir. It won't happen again."

And it didn't. I got the brilliant idea to buy some tapes and a recorder from the PX and sent them off to my parents and siblings. I thought talking was easier than the actual chore of sitting down and writing a letter. I would talk on the tape about whatever was going on in my life. Of course I would never mention what combat was like. I would talk about the other pilots, what I missed for food, maybe the landscape. I would then send it to my brother, who would add his piece then send it on to my other brother and sister, until it finally got to my parents, who now had a little oral collage of everything that was going on with the Chasson family. I personally thought that was a stroke of genius.

With my mom now hearing from me on a regular basis, she didn't worry anymore. I mean, what could happen to me in my new maintenance position?

[19]

NEW GUYS AND NEW

MISSIONS

I WAS PACKING more and more flight time under my belt and
starting to feel pretty good about my skills as a pilot. I wasn't
cocky, but flying a lot of hours every day, week after week, month
after month, things just started to come together. I began flying more
with new guys in the company, trying to teach them what had been
taught to me.

Fortunately for all of us, there was a lull in the war. There would
be the occasional combat assault where we would take fire, but that
was expected. For a while, if I hadn't gotten shot at on a daily basis, I
got worried. If Monday came and went without taking fire, and
Tuesday was like Monday, then I would not look forward to
Wednesday. I figured they were saving it up, so to speak.

During this lull I had several different missions that I had never flown before. One was a psyops mission. the Huey was set up with large loudspeakers and a former Viet Cong, who was now on our side, having seen the error of his ways, installed in the back seating area. We would fly around at 400–500 feet while our newest patriot babbled on about how things were much better with the South Vietnamese Army, things like, "Lay down your arms, no harm will come to you. You will be treated well. You will get money," anything he could think of to get his former comrades to "Chieu Hoi." Chieu Hoi was an initiative started by the South Vietnamese to encourage defection by the Viet Cong and their supporters to the South Vietnamese side during the Vietnam War. I can't say if the program worked, but I can tell you that flying around over Charlie at 400–500 feet was not where I wanted to be. I can only imagine what he was thinking down there, holding his AK-47—"Do I give myself up or shoot down this crazy helicopter that is easy pickings?"

Another seldom-executed mission was flying Agent Orange around. Normally the Air Force would lay down a giant swath of defoliant to take away cover. In a matter of days, the sprayed area was stripped clean of any foliage and therefore any cover. One such case had me flying Agent Orange over the area known as My Lai, a VC-infested area that was a sea of booby traps—what are now called IEDs ("improvised explosive devices"). The thinking was that the defoliated area would expose the enemy so he couldn't ambush ground troops. We had no idea what Agent Orange was or what harmful effects it might have – but if it had such an immediate effect on foliage and vegetation, then what would come from breathing the stuff? Many years later my daughter Katie became very sick. She was weak, could hardly walk and just to touch her she would bruise. I immediately took her to the pediatrician. Her first thought was I was abusing my daughter. Of course that was an emphatic *no*. Her second question was, "Had I ever been exposed to Agent Orange." After days in the hospital Agent Orange was not the source but some other exposure to chemicals was the cause.

Another typical mission was the flare mission. Crews rotated from night to night, flying a Huey loaded with flares, which would burn for maybe a minute as they floated down underneath a small parachute.

One flare would light up an area the size of a football field. This could be a lifesaver for ground troops who thought the enemy was close but, naturally, couldn't see Charlie at night. Flying at night back then was not like it is today with night vision goggles. It was referred to as "unaided." We had no training, but were just told, "Fly to this area, hope that you find it, and start dropping flares until the ground troops tell you that you are in the right area." None of us liked flying at night.

One night I was flying with Cop Williams from the first platoon, headed to the LZ Baldy firebase. The normal routine for a night mission was to fly up the coast to an entry point, then fly directly to the drop point. This was to prevent us from getting shot down by our own artillery, which was usually pretty active at night. I was flying along the coast, trying to keep the villages off my left door so they couldn't shoot at us. Ocean on the right, villages on the left; occasionally there would be lights from a village down below and I would veer to the right to avoid the area. More light, more to the right. At one point after about twenty minutes of "more to the right," I realized that what I thought was a village were actually the lights from small sampans, or fishing boats, working at night. I must have been halfway to Hawaii by the time I figured it out. When I finally made the adjustments and radioed the ground troops, they reported that things were okay for the night and we could return to base.

[20]

SPECIAL FORCES –

AGAIN

I WAS LIVING the good life. Maybe it was because I'd had the same mission before and had some idea what I was doing, or maybe they felt sorry for me, but I got the Da Nang Special Forces mission again. This rotation was to be ten days maximum. Ten days with good food and a nice bed was like a vacation. There were one or two complications but, looking back some forty years later, they have a comical air about them. The first incident happened just outside of the location we flew out of with the Special Forces. The rear area was known as Marble Mountain, just a hair south of Da Nang. It was practically on the ocean, which added to the vacation feeling. We took off from Marble Mountain one day and couldn't have gone more than 500 feet when my crew chief said, "Mr. Chasson, we just lost our door."

I thought there was no way. I was looking right at it. "No," he said, "the cargo door just blew off."

Two thoughts entered my mind. One, how close did it come to the tail rotor? At 500 feet, that would have been a total disaster. Not much you can do without a tail rotor at that elevation. The second thought was, what were we going to do about the door? It was about that time that the crew chief asked, "Do you want to go back and pick it up?"

No way. I remembered the CS grenade we dropped on the village by My Lai and thought the word was out—"Don't give Chasson a second chance."

"No," I said, "we'll just let the villagers down there make a roof out of it or something."

We continued the mission, but I had to let maintenance know what had happened. Did they want to send another door? The decision was to make sure the other door was secure and wait until we got back to the Manor.

The next day, while flying support for an "A" team out in the boonies, I was to make a resupply drop and pick up an injured Vietnamese scout—injured, but not critical. The scout was a twelve-year-old kid who the heat and humidity had gotten to. As I approached, I gave the usual call: "Pistol Pete three-nine, this is Minuteman two-three, over."

The reply was, "Minuteman two-three, this is Pistol Pete three-nine, go ahead."

I said, "I've got resupply for you. Pop smoke, I'm coming in."

"Roger, smoke going out." Within a few seconds I saw a trail of purple smoke waft through the jungle. We called it goofy grape.

"Roger, got your goofy grape. Be there in a minute." Within a few seconds Pistol Pete came back and said, "Uh, Minuteman two-three, we didn't pop goofy grape."

Sure enough, about a klick away a trail of yellow smoke came through the jungle. The VC had been monitoring the radio frequency and popped smoke as well, intending to get us to land to their purple smoke, wait for us to be a few feet off the ground, and that would be the end of Minuteman two-three. The Viet Cong would often capture a radio and smoke whenever they could. Just another potentially deadly incident that now seems almost funny all these years later.

MY LAST EXPERIENCE with the Special Forces was a flight up to an "A" team firebase called My Loc, located on Route 9, just before the famous Rockpile. On this particular day the weather was downright nasty, but I had to get to My Loc at almost any cost, or so I was told. We left Da Nang, low level, following Route 1. I had landmarks learned on my previous experiences up there that I would tick off in my head. My last landmark was Dong Ha, where I would make a left and follow Route 9 to My Loc. I had done it a few times before, but only in good weather. I made one little mistake: I missed Phu Bai, mistook Quang Tri for Phu Bai, then thought Dong Ha was Quang Tri. So I was still flying along at 110 knots or so, looking for Dong Ha so I could make my left turn down Route 9. At the next suspicious landmark, the crew chief yelled out, "Mr. Chasson, this doesn't look right." At that speed we were just about to cross the DMZ. The terrain was a landscape of bomb craters and pretty much nothing else. I made the fastest U-turn I could. The attitude indicator probably showed a sixty-degree bank. I'm sure the North Vietnamese had heard about this crazy guy named Chasson, but even they didn't think he was so crazy that he would fly into North Vietnam.

Backtracking, I finally found Dong Ha and made my way out to My Loc. It was often a series of "woulda, coulda, shouldas" and "forward fumbles" that made the difference for a lot of people in this war. I certainly had my share.

[21]

SNOW REMOVAL

OFFICER

BACK AT MINUTEMAN Manor, nothing had really changed. The command had decided that all warrant officers were to have an extra duty that would occupy their time when they were not flying, so the company commander and first sergeant started passing out jobs. The newest warrants in country got the "shit" jobs, while the old timers got what was left. By the time they got to Fast Eddy Covill and me, the jobs were pretty much all gone, but in order not to offend anyone, they decided Ed would be the flood control officer. I outranked Ed because my name came first alphabetically, so I became the snow removal officer. Of course, it never snowed in Vietnam, although there were days that chilled you to the bone during monsoon season. We were always wet—just being damp would have been a welcome relief. It would have been a relief to change into drier clothes but even our backup clothing would be wet with the humidity.

Both Ed and I thought we would never have anything to do. We were the senior warrant and senior A/C, respectively. But one day the monsoon rains came down in buckets, more than I ever thought possible. The creek next to our hooches began to rise and kept on rising until it put the hooches in danger of being flooded or washed away. What had been a creek in our everyday lives was now a raging river. The wind was whipping and blowing anything that was wasn't tightly secured. At first we all stood around marveling the severe wind, rain, and rising river. Sure enough, this meant that the flood control officer had to act, and quickly. Eddy was out there with a crew filling sandbags and piling them strategically. It was a fight against Mother Nature, and she was winning. I couldn't help myself, and stuck my head out of my hooch.

"Do you know how much snow this would be if it were cold enough to snow?" I said. He only halfway saw the humor in my exclamation as I ducked back inside to drier conditions. A short while later I gave in to help the flood control officer battle the storm. He gave me a look that said "Thanks" and "It's about time."

AFTER A FEW DAYS, the rains let up enough for us to fly. My mission that day was to support the 1st of the 6th Battalion in an area known as Dragon Valley. It was all jungle, with only one or two LZs. It was amazing that ground troops could even move around in there. I called the ground troops for their location and had them pop smoke. There had been no report of enemy activity, so I thought things would be fine.

On short final, we started taking fire. Charlie knew there were only two suitable LZs and probably figured they could just wait for a helicopter to come in to resupply the troops. My crew chief and door gunner immediately returned fire, but not before we had taken hits that killed our hydraulics and hit the damper. I'm not sure if the tradeoff being in charge of my crew's lives and safety outweighed the terror of taking enemy fire. You had no place to hide strapped into your harness. It wasn't like you could lean left or right. You couldn't make yourself smaller hiding behind a glass cockpit. You sat and waited hoping the bullets and terror would cease. On the controls you were somewhat occupied with the flying at hand but the seconds and minutes seemed endless. Trying to control the uncontrollable was only a slight distraction from the extreme fear. Flying a helicopter without hydraulics can be a challenge, but if done very gently and slowly, we could continue to fly. Landing will then often be a running landing, to minimize control movements.

We had two choices—make a running landing at the main Marine airbase, or try a running landing to an area at Minuteman Manor. I elected to try Minuteman Manor for a couple of reasons. One was not tying up the main runway at Chu Lai, and the other was because I thought I had the situation under control. I made a very wide turn to final, and a shallow approach. I think Steve Kerchenfaunt was my peter pilot, and both of us were on the controls. Steve was from Ohio, a tall skinny boy who with an innocent smile eager to learn and ready to follow, putting his faith in those that pretended to know what they were doing. He was not so much shy as hardly ever outspoken. We really had to muscle the controls. It's like driving down the highway when the power steering quits, only worse. We had a major on board, and he was worried that we would all crash and die. He kept asking me whether we were going to make it. I had no real doubts, but he did raise the anxiety level a bit. Steve and I made a perfect running landing, and when the helicopter finally came to a stop, the major was so excited that I thought he was going to kiss us. I think he must have had a bad experience prior to this and was thankful to come out of this one unscathed. The damper that was shot out is now a paperweight on my desk at home.

Another mission I did with Steve was a Long-Range Recon Patrol (LRRP) extraction, deep into "Indian country." I had not been that far west before. It had me thinking we were near Laos. LRRPs would go out on patrols for days, even weeks at a time searching for the enemy, but not always initiating contact. They were tracking them to record movement and strength. As we neared the pre-determined LZ, I called the team on the ground. "Angel Hair three-one, this is Minuteman two-three, over." Silence. Again, I called "Angel Hair three-one, this is Minuteman two-three, over."

I thought I might have the wrong radio frequency and started to try something else when a whisper came back, "Minuteman two-three this is Angel Hair three-one, DANGER CLOSE." This was not good. "Danger close" meant the VC were right on top of them, and they were whispering (What does that tell you?). We had ropes on board as a precaution. We would drop the ropes and the LRRPs would hold on for dear life as we pulled straight up and flew them to safety. Of course, it also meant we had to come out very slowly and fly low, which was never a good thing with the enemy around. But I also had to be high enough so I didn't drag their bodies through the vegetation.

We spotted what might have been the only small clearing they could be in. Close to a mountaintop the jungle was rich in a blanket of triple canopy. I did a "high overhead approach," screaming out of the sky, and settled perfectly in the tiny clearing. There couldn't have been more than a few feet of clearance from the spinning blades. (We didn't use the blades to chop down trees unless we didn't plan on coming out.) I had Steve, the crew chief, and the gunner all calling out the clearance of the spinning rotor and took directions from them to clear the trees. I suppose I had the easy job of setting the Huey down through the opening, while they were frantic in trying to keep me clear. I made it down and in, but not quite down to the ground. I swear there didn't appear to be any clearance between the spinning rotors and trees just waiting to gobble us up. I had an instant thought of crashing my Huey and becoming an instant foot soldier.

It was low enough for the LRRPs to climb up on the skids and be helped in by the crew chief and gunner. But we still had to come out, which meant needing clearance for the blades while expecting to take fire at any second. Sometimes, not getting shot at was worse—the anticipation and expectation would drive us nuts—while actually getting shot at was almost like, "Okay, let's get it over with." Nary a shot was fired, and the LRRPs in back, who looked like they had been out in the boonies for months, not weeks, collapsed on the floor of the Huey, glad to be out of there. When reality set in, they were so grateful that they kept shaking our hands and saying, "Thank you, thank you, thank you."

[22]

SNOWFLAKES

"**G**ETTING SHOT AT was like snowflakes; no two times were ever the same." I came up with this awful analogy while walking to the chow hall with Matt Cummings and a few other guys. We were on a deployment with my unit from the Massachusetts National Guard, while in support of Iraqi Freedom. Matt is one of the nicest, most thoughtful human beings I have ever met. There is nothing he wouldn't do for another human being. (Although, because of my Vietnam connection with Dwight Howard, I might say that Matt is the second nicest person in the world, Dwight being the first. Or maybe they are tied for first. I admire those two immensely.) We had been talking back and forth as we walked to the chow hall when he asked me what getting shot at was like. When I said that, he just about split a gut laughing.

What I meant was each time you get shot at is different, and each time your reaction might be totally different. For example, one day I was flying in and out of a ground unit's location doing resupply. I had no idea if the enemy was close, but I always tried to change things up a little bit. We had been told that, on one previous recon by ground troops, they found a spot where the enemy left behind a crude chalkboard after making a hasty retreat. It showed a random LZ, the wind direction, and the projected flight path a helicopter would have to make, based on the wind and size of the LZ. Charlie was no fool; he was an avid student, learning as much as he could to try to make our lives miserable.

On this particular mission, I had been in and out of the LZ twice, and each time I would vary my approach and takeoff pattern. On the third and final time out, I got to about 1,200 feet and thought there was no longer a need to be extra-careful, so I started to level off. Charlie must have seen this and thought, *I'll teach you!* I heard a faint sound of automatic weapons fire. I could always tell when the bullets were close. The louder the sound—and especially the sharper the crack of the gunfire—the closer the bullet. I didn't always feel impact to the aircraft unless it was a larger caliber than an AK-47. I heard the steady sound of automatic fire, and seconds later rounds were coming through my windshield. When I saw the holes in my windshield, it freaked me out. I got on the radio and started yelling (to no one in particular) that I was taking fire. To me it sounded like the entire Viet Cong and NVA Armies were shooting at me. I got ahold of myself, realized they were just lucky shots, and then played it off like I was John Wayne.

That was the reference I used with Matt, but it didn't come out quite like I intended. My seldom-told stories were usually short. I didn't want to sound different from any other pilot who had flown in Vietnam. But I felt my analogy to Matt warranted further explanation.

[23]

LIFE AT THE MANOR

TIME IN COUNTRY sped by. Every day was filled with flying mission after mission. A day's flight might be as little as six hours or as long as twelve hours. The safety and standardization people said we would be limited to flying a restricted number of hours in a day and maximum of fifteen days in succession. The powers in charge determined there were too many accidents happening due to fatigue. It was one thing to lose pilots, crews, and aircraft to enemy fire, it was another to lose personnel to accidents that might have been avoided if we weren't "dog tired." I learned later in my military career to never try and look ahead to the date or milestone that I was anticipating. Time would never go by as fast as you wanted. It was better to look back on time. Your scheduled R&R was never going to get here but when you look back at an event it would always seem like the time in between was an instant ago.

At the end of that day's flight, if after chow you didn't just hit your cot to get all the rest you could, some of us would gather outside the hooch. Most nights we would sit on our bunker with a beer or two. A bunker was four sandbagged walls, with a sandbagged roof to protect us during incoming rocket attacks. We made a deck out of the top of the bunker and would sit up there pretending we were only miles away from home. Conversations might start out about the individual missions but invariably it would lead to other thoughts. What food would be the first meal you would have? What was my ex-girlfriend doing? Where or what might you be doing if you were stateside? There was some talk about the increase in protests but they hadn't hit the heights they would until the Kent State incident. Some might ask who was running this war, and would we ever "win" the war against communism? There was never a heated argument for one position or the other, it was more to just put your thoughts or opinions out there. We weren't going to settle the world's problems, we didn't have a better battle plan, we just enjoyed being human for a few moments. Just endless ramblings of guys getting ready for the next day. It was all part of the camaraderie.

The incredible bond developed among the people we worked and flew with, day in and day out, is hard to explain. Whether it was in basic training, flight school, flying in the slick platoon, or later on the gunship platoon, we truly were a deep-rooted band of brothers. It was just us. We had to take care of each other, as no one else was going to do it. Al Gore hadn't invented the internet yet so except for the *Stars and Stripes* newspaper with information from home, we were days if not weeks behind. You were almost cutoff from the real world as we called back home. That feeling of isolation contributed greatly to the band of brothers. I think all of us found ourselves out of our comfort zones. Whether it was a different locale or environment, a feeling of isolation or of being alone, it makes you want to bond with those around you.

One of the remarkable things about Vietnam, unlike Iraq and Afghanistan, was the amount of beer that was available. Iraq and Afghanistan offered no such luxury for the everyday soldier. Vietnam was a different war and the PX at Chu Lai was a fairly large warehouse. On a day you weren't scheduled to fly you would probably try and borrow some kind of ground transportation to get to the PX. There was one entire wall occupied by beer, which had to run seventy-five feet long and ten feet high. Budweiser and Schlitz must have sold their souls to the devil because there was an endless supply of beer. After two beers or maybe three, I'd be looking for a nap. I was a lightweight when it came to drinking.

The food was as good as it could be under the circumstances. Still, if you saw a picture of some of us, you'd swear we had been held in captivity for months. Dave Young had the brilliant idea of having a frying pan sent to him, the type that had a cover and dial that went from "warm" to 400 degrees. We started having parents or significant others send canned frosting and cake or brownie mixes and had dessert every night for a while. We also had folks send canned tuna fish and small jars of mayonnaise. That way, we had an entrée and dessert to supplement the food of the mess hall. These little things, though they couldn't make you forget where you were, certainly helped.

OUR COMPANY AREA was at the end of the perimeter, and also at the end of an active runway used by Marine F-4s and A-4s. One day, about mid-afternoon, as two jets took off from the main fixed-wing runway, the lead pilot immediately ran into trouble. His aircraft was going down, and his only options for dumping the large ammo supply onboard were toward the end of the runway or the ocean just off to the left. This was rather an easy decision, so he turned the aircraft towards the ocean and hit his emergency jettison button to bail out before it crashed.

He made it out safely, but the aircraft seemed to have a mind of its own and kept flying. It made a low left turn just before the shoreline. The wingman watched in horror as it headed back towards dry land and Minuteman Manor. His brilliant solution was to shoot his own aircraft down before it could get too far inland. Unfortunately, his angle wasn't quite high enough when he opened fire with his 20mm cannon, and he ended up sending bullets flying through the Manor. Several rounds went through the shower area and made holes as big as baseballs. Fortunately, nobody was in the shower at that time, and thank goodness he adjusted his aim enough to hit his target.

[24]

"DINKS IN THE OPEN"

FLYING WAS FAIRLY routine. We got up in the morning, flew resupply missions for ground units and then whatever other missions the ground troops could think of to give them an edge with the enemy. Most of the flying was at altitudes of 1,500 feet or more. On occasion we would fly up to 10,000 feet to cool off. The temperatures were downright comfortable up there, with the standard lapse rate for temperature. For every thousand feet you went up the temperature would drop three degrees. At 10,000 feet it was downright chilly but a welcome relief. We had to be careful though, as jets never expected to see a helicopter at that altitude.

Just for fun, we used to make landing approaches to clouds. Of course, we would fall right through, but it was just to introduce a bit of variety into the routine. Another flight scenario was "contour flying," treetop-level flying that resembled a roller coaster ride. It was dangerous to be so close to automatic weapons range (with the Huey making that unmistakable sound for miles) and we didn't do it that often. We still needed to practice it though, as it was a maneuver needed in an emergency.

One day, the crew chief and gunner begged me to fly contour back to the firebase of the unit we were supporting. We had a major on board who had flown with me several times, so I thought this wouldn't be all that bad for him, either. I was flying along, trying to instruct my peter pilot in the art of contour flying when the gunner yelled, "We've got dinks in the open." I banked hard-left to pick up several Viet Cong who were just as startled to see us as we were to see them. They took off running, but not before the gunner and crew chief showered M-60 rounds down on them. They hit two, and the other two dropped their packs and disappeared into the vegetation. The major, the intelligence officer for that unit, wanted to land and get the dropped equipment. I wasn't crazy about this idea, but thought, *Okay, one quick trip down to pick up the gear.*

We landed in a rice paddy, and I instructed the crew chief to get the stuff but make it quick. We hadn't gotten all of the VC, and I didn't know how many more there might be. He jumped out and ran for the equipment they had left behind. Just as he picked up the gear, Charlie started shooting at him. I pulled the Huey up to a hover and kicked the tail around to put us between him and where the fire was coming from, which gave the gunner a chance to lay down some cover fire. The crew chief ran for his life and dove headfirst into the cabin area. In a millisecond we were airborne and with the gunner still firing away, I pulled all the collective pitch I could to get out of there.

We made it back to the firebase, LZ Bowman, and dropped the major off, then headed back to the area at the standard 1,500 feet to see if Charlie was still there. The next thing I knew, the major was calling me, asking if I could call Artillery into the area to get some more KIAs. I'd never called in Artillery before, but figured I'd give them the coordinates and they could then give me a "Willy Pete" (white phosphorous tracer) round, so I could adjust fire from that airburst position. All was going okay. I was talking to the major and calling in Artillery fire at the same time. Next thing I knew, I had two F-4 Phantoms asking where I wanted them to drop their 500-pound bombs. I felt like a conductor in a symphony orchestra, trying to coordinate all the different pieces of war. I was definitely multi-tasking and was riding a pretty good high. My adrenaline was racing!

The major called us back to the firebase, and we shut down to debrief. "You'll never believe what we got," he said. There was a radio of big importance, a couple of pistols, a map, and some snorkel tubes (which I thought was a little weird). Then the major said, "Look at this. Does this look familiar to you?" It did. It was a map showing Minuteman Manor, with the locations of all the helicopters and the officers' hooches. He said, "The pistols and radios mean that the Viet Cong we surprised were officers and members of Suicide Sapper Squads." He surmised that they would have used the snorkel tubes to swim undetected up the creek separating our company from battalion and do as much damage as possible before they were spotted. He said, "You and your crew just prevented what certainly would have been a catastrophe." The battalion commander passed this information on to our company commander, who congratulated the whole crew.

He kept most of the items but gave me one of the snorkel tubes. It was rather ingenious—a tube for breathing and two wooden nose clips held together with rubber strips to prevent water from going up through their nostrils. I still have it at home.

NOT FAR FROM the area where we found "dinks in the open" was a valley we called Happy Valley, so named because there was only one way in and the same way out. The Viet Cong pictured us as sitting ducks, which made them very happy. It had very steep terrain and jungle on both sides, so there wasn't much to mask our approach. We joked that when they heard us coming, they would be laughing so hard that they would have trouble getting serious and would just let us fly right in. We also imagined their commander yelling at his troops, "Get serious and shoot that helicopter down."

On one occasion, one of my fellow pilots and crew were on a medevac mission to Happy Valley to pick up a Kit Carson scout (former Viet Cong combatant who had switched sides) who was said to be having trouble breathing. They got shot down on the way in. The call went out that we had an aircraft shot down in Happy Valley. Gunships were scrambled, as well as any other Huey's in the area, to go look for the crew. We hoped that if we could get there quickly the crew had a chance of survival, assuming they made it out of the crash. I arrived after two of my sister airships, so I was flying "high cover." The wreckage was spotted a hundred yards up from the valley floor. It was almost impossible to spot as the helicopter was sitting in the middle of the "triple canopy" jungle. Still intact, it was cradled in the lush vegetation. Triple canopy was jungle at its densest, three layers of palm trees and like vegetation of different heights all trying to reach for sunlight at the top. To the foot soldier traversing the jungle only slivers of sunlight could penetrate to the jungle floor. The crew had actually climbed down to the jungle floor, making their way to the river running through the valley where one of the sister ships picked them up, the gunships covering them all the while. To everyone's relief, all crewmembers were safe, and only ended up with bumps and bruises, which was rather incredible.

We had started to head home when the unit commander called over the radio, "Any Minuteman aircraft in the area, this is Sleeper King six."

I called back, "This is Minuteman two-three, go."

In all the commotion and rescue of the crew, we had forgotten that the ground unit still had a young scout who needed to be medevac'd. As I watched the gunships disappear out of the valley, I said, "Okay, pop smoke. I'm coming in."

I was sure the VC had their sights set on getting a second helicopter. I made it into the cleared-out LZ, which was basically a large bomb crater. I didn't have much room on either side and couldn't get my skids on the ground, so the unit hoisted the young Vietnamese scout into the Huey. With the wounded scout on board, I hadn't taken fire yet, but anticipating it, I pulled the entire collective I had and dropped the bird over into a thirty-degree nose-down altitude. I needed to squeeze every knot of airspeed I could to get out of there and to the hospital as quickly as possible. I was dancing the Huey down the valley, trying not to give the VC a clean shot. To our relief, we made it out of the valley to safer territory.

Then the crew chief said to me, "Mr. Chasson, I think this kid is dead. He doesn't look very good."

I told him to come around from his position and try moving his arms and legs—anything to get him to respond. The scout came to for a minute, but definitely had trouble breathing. I radioed ahead to the hospital and asked for help. "What do I do? He's not breathing." They asked me what my inbound time was to the hospital, and I told them ten minutes.

Ten minutes is too long," they said. "You might need to do an emergency tracheotomy."

I was thinking, *You can't be serious!* They told me what to do, and I gave the controls to Steve, saying, "You got it; keep the needle pegged on max speed."

I was supposed to make a small incision in his throat just above where the collarbone made a small gap, stick a pen in the fleshy part of the cut, and then he should—or might—start breathing again. Just as I was starting to unbuckle, the crew chief said he was breathing again. It was if he knew what was in store for him and thought, *I'm not taking my chances with Chasson.* To my relief, and I'm sure the half-breathing scout's as well, Steve got us to the hospital where crews were waiting to save this young soldier's life.

[25]

DINNER, ANYONE?

U P TO THIS point I haven't mentioned the beauty of Vietnam. While it was more often hot and humid, other times the constant wetness of the monsoon season made it downright cold. It was, however, a luscious green year-round. Chu Lai was on a beautiful beach that stretched for miles, with brilliant white sand and Caribbean blue sea. There were never any local Vietnamese nor hardly a soldier to take advantage of this natural beauty. Up near China Beach in the Danang area it was my understanding they had areas where soldiers could enjoy the sea and surf. The terrain was flat with dunes that maybe reached a height of five feet. My one and only excursion with towel in hand to the water found a perfect temperature for a tired body. From the beach, maybe ten miles inland, mountains would take over from gently rolling hills. At 1,500 feet it was a tropical paradise.

On two occasions, I had a chance to see something almost surreal. For whatever reason I was flying at almost treetop level when we spotted a tiger minding his own business. We started to chase it, but quickly lost the graceful creature in the jungle. It seemed to toy with us, as it dared us to keep up with his agile gait and long strides. This creature seem to cover ten feet with every leap. Sadly, I'm told there have been no tigers reported in Vietnam since 1990.

The second surreal moment was when we surprised a deer in a wooded area. As soon as we saw it, the crew chief and gunner could think of nothing but "venison for dinner." I gave the go ahead for them to surprise the platoon with dinner. All went fine until we went down to pick up our meal. As we were loading the animal on board, the Viet Cong in the area were watching us and decided it was their meal instead of ours, and we started taking fire. I had two crewmembers hauling a dead deer into the aircraft and nobody manning the machine guns. I was not a fan of venison anyway, so I pulled pitch to get out of there, dinner or no dinner. Somehow though they managed to get the deer on board and we headed home with steaks for all. Sometimes the little things helped us forget where we were.

[26]

A PERFECT "HIGH

OVERHEAD"

I T WAS SAID that the Army owned the day and the Viet Cong, the night. In My Lai, however, the Viet Cong owned both day and night. It was heavily populated and, for the most part, the villagers were either pro-VC or lived in total fear of them. If they sympathized with the Americans the VC would kill them. Conversely if they sympathized with the VC, the Army would hold them responsible. That was one of the main reasons why the My Lai massacre happened. The VC owned the whole area. The My Lai episode was a search and destroy mission initiated and executed by the Army. Five hundred women and children were slaughtered, some raped before they were killed. There could have been more casualties except for the heroics of a lone helicopter working in the area that saw what was going on. Warrant Officer Hugh Thompson landed his scout helicopter to plead with some of the ground troops to help him save as many villagers he could.

Unless you've walked in the boots of an 11-Bravo infantry soldier through the endless area of booby traps and mines, watching fellow soldiers disappear in front of you, it's hard to realize what they faced day in and day out. I would imagine it wouldn't take much for a soldier to react in a way he normally wouldn't. It could have been a series of events that led up to the massacre. Like pulling a loose thread on a sweater, it just couldn't or wouldn't stop unraveling. Murder can never be excused, the massacre can never be justified or rationalized. It was a senseless taking of life and later determined the fault of the chain of command.

A few months later, we had a combat assault into a small landing zone there, only large enough for three Huey's at a time. The insertion went off without a problem, and I was assigned to be the unit's resupply helicopter for the day. That LZ was just a hundred yards off the beach, so on my first approach I came in from the ocean, knowing the Viet Cong Navy wasn't around. No problems in, no problems out. The next approach, I came in fast and low, again with no problems. On the third trip in, I was carrying the finance officer (a lieutenant for the company). It was payday and vouchers had to be signed. This time I started my approach from the "high overhead" position, as much for the practice as anything. I made a beautiful three-turn dive into the LZ, screaming out of the sky at 2,500 feet per minute. As I touched down, I thought to myself, *That was a thing of beauty.*

Just as the skids kissed the ground, however, I heard "crack crack." At first I thought the blades might be hitting a stray leaf from a tree, but with another "crack," I knew we were taking fire. We were relatively light, and I nearly over-torqued that bird getting out of there. As I was pulling pitch two soldiers who were walking up to the aircraft were hit by ground fire. I watched them fall to the ground. Within seconds, the lieutenant in the back was hit, as well as my gunner, who was hit bad. My arm went flying off the collective as I took a hit to the left arm. I said, rather calmly but angrily, "I'm hit."

My peter pilot, Andy Johnson, grabbed the controls to take over, but I wasn't giving up anything. The shock had subsided, and now reality was sinking in. There was so much blood all over the cockpit and windshield from the lieutenant's wounds that I almost had to fly sideways to see where I was going. I was gripped with rage that everything that seemed so perfect about the flight had gone terribly wrong. I did everything tactically correct. I called out to my crew asking if everyone was okay.

There was no response from my door gunner, Brownie. I looked back to see him slumped over his M-60. Thinking he might fall out, I yelled to the crew chief, "Get him secure!" My immediate reaction was that I got Brownie killed. He lifeless body seemed suspended, poised to fall out except for his shoulder harness. I had failed to safeguard my gunner's life. Dave Adams was my crew chief, and I flew with him quite a bit. He was a young blonde from the mid-west. Normal in stature as to height and weight but oh so eager to do whatever he could to make everyone around him at ease. He scurried around to check on the gunner and made sure he wasn't falling out. Unfortunately he was unconscious. Dave then tried to stop the lieutenant's bleeding as best as he could. I was pissed at the ground unit. This should not have happened. I called the resupply LZ and said, "Your guys may have just gotten two people killed. The rest of the unit was walking around like it was a day at the beach instead of securing the LZ."

I flew down the coast with the needle pegged on 124 knots, heading for the hospital. We got there in less than seven minutes. I knew that every second mattered. We landed and I had Captain Johnson shut her down while I raced to the side of the aircraft where medics were putting my gunner on a gurney. The lieutenant was being taken care of, so my focus was on my gunner.

The medics started working on the bullet wound to his leg while the nurse asked him what his name was, his ID number, and the like. Seeing the bullet wound to his head, I was having trouble understanding why they weren't working on that wound instead of asking him stupid questions. I said to the nurse, "I'll give you that information, just fix his head!"

I don't think she got the gist of what I was trying to say because when I didn't know the answer to one of her questions, she again started to ask the gunner. In one motion, I grabbed her by both shoulders and, putting her eyes about three inches from the gaping hole in his head, said, "Look, he has a bullet in his head! See that hole right there?"

I relaxed my hold and she stood upright, saying, "Doctor, you'd better take a look at this." Then she looked at me and said, "You've been shot."

I looked where she was looking, thinking, *Oh yeah, I remember now.* I still had fragments of the bullet in my arm from where it ricocheted off the sliding chicken plate. It had come from my aircraft's 4-o'clock position and missed my head by about a foot. She had me come with her to another doctor to be treated. I apologized to her, saying I was just worried about my gunner. She said not to worry, stress does funny things to people.

They patched my arm up, and I went outside to inspect the battle damage to the aircraft. Andy had gone over it pretty closely with the crew chief Dave, and even though we all decided it was safe to fly back, I was a little reluctant, as I didn't want to get into trouble again with the battalion commander.

After the initial impact of the bullet, getting shot felt like someone was cutting my skin open with a very hot dull knife. The skin felt like it was slowly being ripped off my arm. They gave me a Novocain shot and preceded to stitch me up. They also gave me pain pills for later, if needed. I was pretty tired, so later that night I took some of the pills to ease what pain there was. Any time we took medicine we had to be cleared by the flight surgeon before we could fly again. This meant that the next day I would be off, which was okay with me because I wanted to check on my gunner at the hospital.

I went first to the PX to get some magazines, hoping they would be of some comfort in his recovery. Sadly, Brownie was pretty much a vegetable. The bullet rendered him speechless and probably unable to hear, as it had exited just under his ear. The doctor didn't know if he would be able to walk again, but they were transferring him to Japan and the hospital network there. I squeezed his hand and said I was sorry this happened, that it was my fault. I want to say he understood, but I'll never know, there was no visual or physical response to my words or touch.

With that, I went to see how the lieutenant was doing—better than Brownie, I hoped. I found him lying in bed with his leg heavily wrapped and suspended. The bullet had hit an artery, which explained why there had been so much blood in the cockpit. He was going to be okay. I think "red-lining" the aircraft for max speed saved some precious seconds. We talked for a bit. I told him he was lucky he was going home and left the magazines for him. He thanked me for getting him out of there, and I said I was just trying to get out of there myself, he just happened to be on board. As I said goodbye, I felt good about having visited. I might have been the only contact he had, as his unit was still in the bush.

[27]

ALL ABOARD

THERE WAS AN area the 196th Infantry Brigade worked exclusively around this time. It was just north of Tien Fuck, which pretty much sums up the kind of area it was. It was comprised of LZ West and LZ East. Geographically, it was a valley from Laos that just dumped into the area. It was basically the NVA's highway to the southern half of I Corp. There was an identifiable landmark we used for navigation purposes. We called it "Million-Dollar Hill" because, during a combat assault, four Hueys on landing were shot down on the spot. At $250,000 per aircraft in 1969, it was aptly named.

On one particular day, while the war was heating up in this area, I was assigned along with another ship to evacuate residents from a village that was in line with the expected movement of the NVA. In and out of this small village, we kept picking up people and shuttling them to Tam Ky, a district province about thirty miles away. The day was ending fast, with little sunlight and fuel left for the mission. I was the last bird in, and therefore the only hope of getting out before the spring offensive started for anyone remaining. We landed and were rushed by a crowd of women and children in a panic to get aboard. The crew chief and gunner kept shoving them in, then said, "That's it, Mr. Chasson, we're full."

I asked, "Are there anymore wanting to get out?"

"Yes," came the reply.

I still had some room up front, and said, "I can take a couple of small ones up front, sitting on the center pedestal."

As I said, we were light on fuel, but coming out of there I still had to pull maximum torque. My passengers were all women and children, and the crew and I felt good about getting them out.

I hoped that someday they would be able to get back home but didn't have a great deal of faith that it would happen. We landed at Tam Ky, and twenty-three women and children got off that Huey. At first, I thought the crew chief and gunner were playing a joke on me—having the women walk around to the other side of the helicopter, climb in, then climb out again. It was something you might see at the circus with the clowns.

"Nope," the crew chief said, "Twenty-three is what we had."

[28]

LITTLE OF THIS, LITTLE OF THAT

THERE WAS A mess hall server/cleaner named Kim who would come over to my hooch in the afternoon and talk. We may have kissed a bit, but she was smarter than I was, so that's as far as it went. From her I learned a few words of Vietnamese. There were the old standbys, "I love you," "You're very pretty," and, "Give me a cigarette." The rest was slang like *didi mau*, meaning "Get out of here fast," *dinky dau*, which meant you were crazy, and the often-used "Me love you long time, GI." "Love you long time" was code for "Get me out of this place and take me to America." I often wondered what happened to Kim when the North Vietnamese took control of the country. Did she go on with her life? Was she able to find a way out of Vietnam to the United States? As for so many of the Vietnamese, it was never her war.

I HAD AN odd nighttime mission one night. Nights without any kind of illumination made flying very difficult. My orders were to fly to a predetermined grid and identify it from the air. It was a bend in a river that came out of Happy Valley. I was in contact with a Navy controller on the ground. Once I determined that I was, in fact, at the right location, I was to back off to a safe distance while an A-6 from the Navy would bomb this particular site to little pieces.

The river was an aquatic highway for the Viet Cong, used to transport weapons and supplies to their comrades near populated areas. There were a couple of things wrong with this plan from my point of view. First, it was pitch black. Trying to find the location while using a map in the dark was difficult. Second, I was flying around at 500 feet over an area that we already knew had bad guys on the ground. Fortunately, I found the designated area and backed off as instructed so the A-6 could drop a number of 500-pound bombs. The idea was that if I could determine they were successful, they could use this tactic again, so after the bombing pissed the enemy off, I was to go back in and recon the battle damage. No worries, right?

The trouble was, after the "all clear to go back in" was given, I couldn't find the area again. I flew around and around looking for the same turn in the river but couldn't find it. I was thinking, *Here I am at 500 feet, prime AK-47 range, in an area where the enemy are really upset that they have just been bombed.* After about ten minutes or so, the crew and I were starting to feel we were really pushing our luck. I made the command decision to get the hell away from the area and climb to altitude. I finally called the Navy ground controller and said, "Yup, you got it, right on the money. We are so outta here." Much to the crew's relief, we didi maued out of there, not giving a thought to the accuracy of future radar-controlled bombing missions.

IT WASN'T UNCOMMON for an A/C who was getting "short" (within thirty days or so of going home) to call for a little help if his mission was getting hot. One such mission happened to John Johnston. He was trying to take soldiers out of an LZ that had been attacked by a swarm of hornets. He wasn't begging off the mission, just asking for help from anybody in the area.

I heard the call and said I would be right there, then asked what the situation was. A platoon of grunts, trying to climb a hill, had encountered a swarm of hornets, and the commander on the ground was desperate. I spotted John's Huey just coming out of a hillside LZ and started my approach into the same spot. On "short final" I realized this wasn't going to be as easy as I had thought. The LZ was small, and the slope of the hill made actual touchdown impossible. I came back around for another approach and settled into a hover with one skid a couple of feet from the ground, and the other about five feet off the ground. I was afraid that someone was going to walk into the spinning rotor on the upslope of the hill.

The bees were swarming so bad that someone on the ground decided to "pop smoke" to irritate the bees, hoping they would scatter and leave the area. It did irritate the bees, but they didn't leave, and now I was hovering in a very tight LZ with purple smoke in and around my cockpit, making visibility poor. I was holding the bird as steady as I could as the center of gravity shifted with each grunt jumping on board. Two dogs that were also attacked by the swarm were desperate to get out of there as well. We were at max weight with the troops and dogs, yet it was effortless to just fall off the side of the mountain and be in immediate transitioning lift for flight.

Naturally, adding to the anxiety, we took some small-arms fire as we were leaving. It couldn't have been just a simple medevac. As we flew to the rear area of the unit where there was an aid station, I looked back at some of the ground troops. Their faces were swollen to the point of almost unrecognizable features. Even the dogs were disfigured. I've said any given day in Vietnam could present some weird flights, this was a perfect example.

THERE WAS ANOTHER strange incident involving ground troops. We had taken to carrying grenades and eventually 60mm mortars onboard the aircraft. We went back and forth as to whether we should carry this ordnance or not. We felt like we had our own Air Force. Although they weren't 500-pound bombs, we still felt we could do some damage. If we lined the Huey up with a target on the ground, flying at 1,500 feet and 80 knots, when the target came between the pilot's pedals, we would call out to the crew chief to drop the mortar or grenade. I could hit within fifty feet of a target every time.

One day, I got a call from a ground unit asking, "Any Minuteman aircraft in the area? This is Willow Tree six."

"This is Minuteman two-three, go."

The radio operator relayed from his commander that he had "enemy elephants" in sight. I wasn't aware that the enemy had elephants, but I did know they were very clever and would utilize anything they had to make their life easier. I knew that they used water buffalo to transport weapons and equipment, but the use of elephants was a first. He gave me approximate directions and distance to the elephants and asked if I could drop some ordnance on them. This sounded like fun, and we headed out to help. We were looking and looking for the elephants when he said, "You're right on top of them."

The crew and I still didn't see any elephants, but I told the crew chief to get ready to drop a mortar and the ground commander could adjust fire from there. Sure enough, we dropped a round, got an explosion, and he came back over the radio saying, "You've got it, you're right on target; bring some thunder." I came around to have a look and the only thing I saw was a gigantic rock formation.

I called Willow Tree six and said, "Are you sure I got it?"

"Yes," he answered.

I said, "Well, we just blew up a very large rock."

Nothing but silence. I'm sure from his vantage point it had looked suspicious, and he and his platoon thought they were going to be the heroes of the company, but the butt of jokes was all they were going to be now.

Word eventually came down from headquarters that there would be no more carrying ordnance of any kind. A stray AK-47 round could hit one of the grenades or mortars and that would be lethal. We also heard that an aircraft from our sister company made a fatal mistake while transporting a prisoner to a detention center. Like many other helicopters at the time, they were carrying grenades on board, and in flight, the VC grabbed one of the grenades and pulled the pin. The helicopter exploded in mid-air, with all crewmembers lost.

[29]

AUSTRALIA R&R

WHILE STATIONED IN-COUNTRY, we had the opportunity to spend seven days at a time in one of several areas deemed safe for ground troops. Hawaii was very popular with married men and guys who had a longtime girlfriend. Since Aileen had given me the boot and the brief fling with Linda only lasted maybe two weeks, there was no longtime girlfriend for me.

One type of seven-day period was known as "rest and recuperation" or "R&R," and the other was just called a "seven-day leave." Basically, they were the same thing, except with R&R we were guaranteed to get our choice of destinations, while the other was on a first-come, first-serve basis. When the time came for my "R&R," I chose Australia because I was eager to see women with "round" eyes. In Vietnam, ninety percent of the women we had contact with had sloped eyes. It's not that they weren't attractive, they just didn't look "American." Australia presented the opportunity to see women who closely resembled American women.

The freedom bird landed in Sydney, and we had a briefing on the potential dangers of scams, kidnappings, women, and STDs. Once released we were on our own, and I had no idea what to do next. I headed for downtown Sydney, just walking around, and I ended up in a park in the middle of the city. I was just sitting there minding my own business when a group of four Australians walked by. One of the girls smiled at me and said, "Hi." I was still in uniform, and for a second wondered if she was talking to me. Surprised, I replied with an awkward, "Hi."

They kept walking, and I assumed that was the end of our conversation. I had just finished my cigarette (I had fibbed to God when I told him I would quit smoking if he got me out alive on my flight with Barry Lamkin at Tien Fuck) and gotten up when the same group of guys and girls came by again. I can't remember what she said to me, but my reply in an American accent made her stop. She walked over, much to the dismay of the others in her group, and we started talking. The next thing I knew she had invited me to walk with them. I got a strange look from the guys, but the girls were all very friendly. After another thirty minutes I was alone with this round-eyed Australian, who was rather attractive regardless of whether someone had been in Vietnam for seven months. We walked and talked, and soon enough she helped me find a hotel across from Coogee Beach. It wasn't summertime, so it was just a hotel with a pretty view. The weather and the threat of sharks meant no one would be swimming.

Kings Crossing was the local hot spot, with restaurants and bars galore. We spent several intimate days together before she suggested we head up to her "mum's," about an hour's train ride north. I got to see more of the countryside, which was nice. I was glad to be able to say, "I've seen Australia." At the end of my R&R she promised she would write and needed my address. I wrote it on a fifty-dollar bill, which was all I had. "No worries," she said, and assured me she would be writing. Yup, I never heard from her.

Five months later I was due for my seven-day leave, and off to Australia I went again. This time I was savvier about Sydney and the nightlife in Kings Crossing. I was in a bar, sipping on a beer when *bam!* There she was, the same beautiful Australian girl. She said, "Oh, I was going to write, but I lost that piece of paper you wrote your address on." Well, you know what they say—fool me once, shame on you; fool me twice... I didn't care. Except seven wonderful days later she had given me a souvenir that I didn't want to bring back to the Manor with me. Upon landing, it was straight off to the flight surgeon for me. He didn't know what I had, but after learning of my seven-day leave in Australia his remedy was to tell me to place my hands on the two painted silhouettes on the wall and get ready for a "two-cheek shot" of penicillin.

The painted hands on the wall were a funny touch. It told me I was not the first, and I wouldn't be the last.

PART 3:

THE PLAN

[30]

BACK IN THE COCKPIT

DURING THE WAR, 154,000 soldiers were hospitalized for wounds. Ninety-nine percent of those who made it through the first twenty-four hours survived. Another one million soldiers were medevac'd. The average time from battlefield to hospital was twenty minutes once the call came in and the wounded soldier had been stabilized on the battlefield. Every pilot put medevac missions first, under any and all circumstances.

After my "two cheek shot," it was only a day before I was back to "left-seating it," as we would sometimes say, and flying *slicks,* which meant that we could end up doing just about anything. Medevac was the most rewarding, but there were designated medevac units (which we called "dustoffs") that, if available, were the ones to take those missions. Occasionally, a dustoff couldn't be there for a priority mission without putting the wounded soldier at much greater risk. Time was always key. The call came out one day for an emergency medevac. A general call for anybody meant two things: one, the soldier or soldiers were critical, and two, the LZ was going to be hot, no time to wait for usual medevac helicopter. I quickly turned to my crew and asked, "Are you guys willing to do this?"

Without hesitation, my crew, in unison, responded with an emphatic "Yes," even knowing full well there would be no gunship protection. This was a different crew that I was flying with so I wanted them to have the chance to say no. I don't recall their names or faces just the emphatic, "Yes let's do this."

I called the ground soldiers and said, "Minuteman two-three is six minutes out. Pop smoke." The unit warned that the LZ was hot, and said he had two critical and three dead. I came back saying, "Give me the wounded now, and I will get the dead later."

"Roger that."

I then told him I would be on the ground no more than thirty seconds, so it would have to be fast. I came in at treetop level from the only direction I could, based on his instructions. I almost overflew the LZ, but then I spotted the wounded and banked the Huey hard-left with almost no lift left in the blades. We plopped down, right next to the wounded, hitting hard enough that the bird sort of bounced on the ground. Between the first bounce and the second, the troops on the ground threw their wounded mates on board and signaled me to get out of there. There was no need for a third bounce, as I was already pulling all the pitch I had and heading out.

As I started to fly off to the right, the ground radio operator started yelling, "Two-three, don't go right, don't go right." I turned to the left, and again he was yelling, "Two-three, don't go left, don't go left."

He hadn't left me with a lot of choices, so I headed for the "clown's mouth" and hoped and prayed for the best. The best is what I got, and although we took heavy fire, the crew thought things went surprisingly well, and I should do that move more often if the need arose. The wounded were critical, so I stayed low-level to save time. I had Steve radio ahead to the hospital to let them know we were coming. Deciding that detouring around the main fixed-wing airbase would waste too much time, I called the tower and said, "Chu Lai Tower, this is Minuteman two-three. I've got priority medevac on board, clear the airspace." I had the needle pegged to the max. The tower immediately cleared the airspace of any incoming aircraft, and we flew past the tower in a blur.

Once we arrived at the hospital, we checked out the bird and decided we needed to replace this damaged aircraft for a bullet-hole-free model. Getting stuck at the hospital waiting for maintenance recovery was not a bad way to spend some time. Eventually we were able to head back to Minuteman Manor for another aircraft.

Upon return, the ground unit said the enemy had broken contact and the other wounded had been evacuated, but could we take out the dead? It was important to get these fallen soldiers out, and definitely a more solemn occasion. It was a longer, quieter ride to what they called "graves registration," where we ended up taking the dead. Every time I came into graves registration I thought of the soldiers who were working that job and what it must be like for them, day after day, handling dead bodies. I didn't know how they could get used to that. The dead soldiers I would see were few. Most of my missions involved getting wounded to a hospital, to one day be whole. The rare occasions I had to pick up the dead for transport were always a solemn and eerily quiet ride. I would pull pitch from the landing pad at graves registration and leave all the death behind. The soldiers who worked there could not leave. Everyday more helicopter's would arrive, more bodies, an endless supply. How did they deal with those emotions, day in and day out?

[31]

More of "This and That"

NOT LONG AFTER, my crew and I were flying support for a unit working the My Lai area. We got a call from the unit saying that they had spotted a Caucasian male running with a Viet Cong squad about two klicks away. They wanted me to try to verify if, in fact, this Caucasian was working with the enemy, or if he had been captured. There had been no reports of an American soldier missing, maybe this Caucasian-looking individual was Russian.

The VC disappeared the minute they heard my blades whopping in the air. I told the ground unit I was going to call in artillery fire on the last known position. Normally I didn't have too much trouble with this, but this time the radio operator and I weren't on the same page. Usually I would give the artillery guys the coordinates, then I would ask for a Willy Pete that would air burst in the general area. With that,

I could adjust fire onto the target and not endanger any others who might be in the area.

The artillery unit didn't want to waste time with the Willy Pete, they just wanted to fire for effect. Basically, they didn't want the Caucasian, whether a Russian or an American helping the other side, to get away. Their thought was, *We're ready, let's do it now.* I was trying to make sure we had the same gun target line so that the rounds could land where I wanted them and not on the American unit I was working with. I thought we had communicated the specifics of the gun target line, but something just didn't seem right. They were going to use three tubes, "full fire for effect," when I yelled, "Cease fire, cease fire!" To my relief and that of the ground unit I was supporting, no rounds were fired.

The ground unit came over the radio and said, "Two-three, this is Diamond Mike six: something doesn't sound right with their gun target line."

That was my thought as well, and I didn't want any American casualties because of miscommunication or a stupid mistake. Later, I also thought, *What if the Caucasian was an American prisoner?* I didn't know for sure, but I thought his chances of survival were better than they would have been after raining down a whole lot of whop. After deciding to abandon the fire mission, the unit on the ground wanted us to transport a prisoner they had captured back to the detention center. I called Diamond Mike six to make sure that the prisoner was securely tied up. I wasn't carrying any ordnance, but I didn't want some suicidal VC to grab a weapon and bring down our helicopter.

We landed, got the prisoner on board, and took off for the detention center. Apparently, my idea of a prisoner being securely tied up and Diamond Mike six's were two very different concepts. I looked back at the prisoner and thought, *This is not going to work.* His hands were tied with what might have been dental floss, and there was no blindfold. I said to my peter pilot, "You take the controls." I turned around, took out my .38 pistol, put the end of the barrel about six inches from his head, and in words he couldn't possibly understand said, "Don't move, motherfucker. I will blow your head off if you move one inch. I am more nervous than you are, so don't move."

He must have thought, *Oh God, this is that crazy guy Minuteman two-three.* Whether he understood my words or not, he must have gotten my point because he didn't move. Then again, I never dropped my pistol from his head for the entire ride. I was never so relieved to get to the detention center, and I'm sure that the VC was also happy and relieved to get to a detention center and away from me. At least we weren't a mid-air explosion.

WHEN WE COULD, we were always watching or listening on the radio for other crews from the 176th who were flying that day. One day while working down in the southern part of the AO, things were really heating up in the northern sector and most of the aviation assets were redirected up there. CPT Marv Adams needed to go into an LZ that was probably going to be hot, and there was no gunship protection for him. He made a blind call to any Minuteman aircraft, and I responded, "Minuteman two-six, this is Minuteman two-three, over."

He explained the situation and the location. Our plan was that he would go into the LZ while I would fly about 500 feet above him, trying to draw whatever enemy fire I could. Neither one of us was in a good position. As he made his approach, I came in behind him. I let him settle into the LZ and stayed at 500 feet, which was perfect killing range for the enemy. I was circling overhead, willing him to hurry up. The anticipation of these moments resulted in nothing less than acute stress. Marvin knew the dangers we were both in and was out of there in probably thirty seconds, but those were the longest thirty seconds I could remember. He came out and we headed back to the rear area together with no shots fired, much to our surprise.

AS I'VE MENTIONED, we would let our crew chiefs fly up front from time to time. One of our most trusted LZ coordinators at LZ Baldy, who would do anything for us, asked if he could fly. He never got a chance to fly, even as a passenger, because he was always at the LZ organizing the resupply going out or personnel coming in. I asked the rest of the crew, and they said, "Sure, why not?"

He started to climb in the back, but I told him to come on up front. After I gave a few quick instructions, we took off from the LZ with a few South Vietnamese soldiers on board we were taking to a CAP location. Everything was going smoothly. The LZ coordinator was doing a pretty good job, although my hands were always close to the flight controls.

We had been flying for about ten minutes when I started to smell smoke. I asked the crew chief and gunner if they could see anything, but they said no. I could still smell smoke, and I knew it wasn't my imagination. A few minutes later the crew in the back started to smell the smoke as well. The crew chief suddenly yelled that one of the South Vietnamese had lit some kind of hibachi grill and was trying to cook something. I couldn't believe it, what in the world was going through his head?

Now, I had two options: put the Huey down in unknown territory with a non-rated person in the other seat and put out the fire, or try to keep flying to the CAP site, put out the fire, then shoot the moron who started the fire. I elected to land right away because I couldn't be sure that the wind whistling around inside the aircraft wasn't going to set something important on fire. Besides, there would have been witnesses at the CAP if I shot the moron. I also knew that, for the LZ coordinator, this was going to be the highlight of his tour in Vietnam.

[32]

GETTING SHORT

I WAS "GETTING short." My time in Vietnam was coming to an end. Up to this point I had survived twelve months, flying nearly 1,200 hours, and I was happy to be going home. There would be another Aileen, I hoped, and I would have fooled Linda by coming back alive.

Unlike World War II, GIs returning from Vietnam did not receive a hero's welcome, but at least I would be going home alive. I would be leaving men I had lived and bonded with during a period of extreme circumstances. I would be leaving Cheetah, Dave Young, and Steve Kerchenfaunt. We were brothers in arms, misfits of sorts, which made the daily grind of flying and dying almost bearable. We didn't have much then but we had each other, and although there is no contact anymore, I will never forget those with whom I served. There is a Vietnam Helicopters Pilot Association that has a reunion every year in cities throughout the country. From everything I've heard it is well received, but I have never been. At this point in my life I don't really have the desire. Perhaps early on but not anymore. That's just me, I can't fully explain it nor understand why I feel that way. My remembrance of my comrades may be a little blurred but you don't forget.

Returning home, television shows seemed to portray every Vietnam returnee as some kind of psychopath or natural-born criminal. In some instances this may have been true. During the 60s, many judges when sentencing criminal cases, gave young men a choice: go to jail or join the military, which surely meant going to Vietnam. I'm sure at the time, enlisting seemed the lesser of two evils. Who knows, did they have a proclivity to be a career criminal or did the war just make them one? Of course, it's just as likely that this portrayal made for better television, for Hollywood. There wasn't the acronym of PTSD that you could pin on a soldier's misfortune. It was there in all its horrible glory but not understood. It was real in World War I, it will be real in every conflict we ever have. It's better understood and treated today, but it will always be a horrible side-effect of combat. Today's military does not accept the civilian rejects anymore—or certainly not as it did in the 60s. Even an arm full of tattoos is reason for rejection.

I was determined to keep a very low profile, and just try to "let go and let God." I would put Vietnam behind me. The strange part of returning from Vietnam was that it signaled an end to that significant part of my life. One day I'm a pilot, flying missions and being shot at. Next day, instead of trudging through a rice paddy from a burning helicopter, I'm walking through Boston Commons as though the war never existed. What could be more surreal than that?

I HAD APPROXIMATELY ten days left in-country. Prior to the expected return date, or DEROS, I filled out a "dream sheet," which was a chance to pick three places where I hoped to get stationed on my next assignment. I went out on a limb and chose Fort Hamilton, NY; someplace in Thailand; and anywhere in Germany. Go figure, what I got was Fort Hunter-Stewart in Georgia. I was to be an instructor pilot and teach South Vietnamese how to fly. I also had to be able to communicate with them. With my limited command of Vietnamese and their limited command of English, I had serious reservations about this new position. I had made it through Vietnam alive but now feared this could be the end of me! While on R&R in Australia, I had also filled out an application for Air America, which was an aviation wing of the CIA. I had heard that they were paid on either the degree of difficulty of the mission or at what altitude they flew. I thought I could do this for a year or so, bankroll some money, and then get on with my life. Unfortunately, I heard back at a later date with a, "We are not looking at the moment, but we'll let you know."

With ten days to go, I prepared for a combat assault that should have been a piece of cake. It was a three-ship lift into LZ Minuteman, with gunship coverage. *No worries*, I thought. The troops we were carrying were ARVN soldiers, otherwise known as the Army of the Republic of South Vietnam. There was a disparity in transporting ARVN soldiers, American soldiers, and the Vietnamese Montagnard soldiers that we did some work with while flying with the Special Forces. American troops would jump off the helicopter the second the skids kissed the ground as we came into a LZ. The Montagnard soldiers would jump off maybe five feet before the skids hit the ground. In both cases, the smart troops wanted to get as far away from the prime target—the helicopter—as possible. With the ARVN soldiers (who were still "dinks" to us), we almost had to beat them with a stick to get them off the helicopter.

LZ Minuteman sat on top of a very small knoll that was exposed on all four sides. The lead Huey started the approach, and I was in chalk two position. Everything went well, right up to the skids touching the ground. Seemingly out of nowhere, I heard a huge explosion and felt the Huey rock from one skid to the other. "What in the world was that?" I thought. At the same time, we started taking AK-47 fire from our 3 o'clock position. I jumped on the radio and started yelling, "Taking fire, taking fire, 3 o'clock."

The lead gunship pilot was Tom Mellon, who had come in-country about the same time as Fast Eddy Covill and me. He was on my tail and immediately started laying down 2.75 rockets on my 3 o'clock. So, I had this huge explosion that had just gone off to my left and was taking AK-47 fire from my right while Tom was laying down a series of rockets on my right that were so close they were shaking the earth beneath my skids. All that with less than ten days to go.

As this was going on, the other two aircraft in the formation could not leave the LZ. We all had to go at once so the gunships could cover us. I was ready to *didi mau* out of there, but I had one ARVN soldier who wouldn't get off my helicopter. I turned around and tried to beat him with whatever I had, when my crew chief, Dave Adams said, "Mr. Chasson, that guy has been shot."

"Oh, well. He can stay on board, I guess."

To the relief of the other two ships, I called "Two-three is ready," and we pulled pitch to get the hell out of there. We got to an altitude of maybe fifty feet off the LZ, and Dave says, "Uh, Mr. Chasson."

"What is it, David?" I said, with a bit of attitude and disbelief at what had just happened.

"I've been shot too," he replied, almost apologetically.

"Oh, shit," I said, and immediately dove off to the right. Before I had a chance to tell the rest of the flight what was going on, I was diving out of the sky. They assumed I was going down because of ground fire and started yelling to me, "Two-three, are you all right? What's going on?"

"I'm going to the hospital. My crew chief has been hit, and I've got wounded on board."

It was a ten-minute flight to the 27th Med Hospital. I maneuvered the bird off to the side of the helipad and shut it down while the hospital staff came running out. They got Dave inside and discovered his legs had several holes—I say *holes* because after further review of the helicopter, we determined what had happened. Those clever Viet

Cong had booby-trapped the LZ with a claymore mine, triggered to go off as I touched down. If lead had landed fifteen feet short of the actual point of landing, the blast would have taken out a whole lot more people. As it was, the detonation went off at about our 7 o'clock position, instead of 9–10 o'clock. It was another "oh shit," that could easily have been an "oh fuck" moment.

We called maintenance to take a look at my sick bird and see if it was flyable. Although the previous battalion commander had left, I did not forget my lesson from Tien Fuck.

"Nope," they said, "We will have to sling-load it out of here."

The maintenance officer said, "I stopped counting at fifty," referring to the number of BB holes from the claymore booby trap.

I went in to check on Dave. He was doing all right. It's amazing, the power of morphine. I told him, "You have a million-dollar wound and will be going home before me, you lucky bastard."

A million-dollar wound was one that was serious enough to send you home, but not so debilitating that it would ruin your life. He joked that he was halfway to me, referring to the number of purple hearts that I had. I said, "And that's the way we are going to keep it, for both of us."

WHILE BACK AT Minuteman Manor, I finally had a chance to reflect and had a revelation: that was it. I wasn't taking any more chances flying in Vietnam. I was inside ten days, and as far as I was concerned my flying time was over. I had earned it, and in my mind I deserved it. What company commander would want my death, inside of ten days, on his conscience?

I did have a little leverage, as I was the old guy and we weren't that short of pilots. Seems weird to say I was the "old guy" at twenty-two. (Think about what you were doing, or will be doing, at twenty-two.)

The commander agreed with my platoon leader. I could pack up and help out in operations for the next several days.

[33]

AN OFFER YOU CAN'T

REFUSE

J UST THREE DAYS before I was to go home, they made me
an offer I couldn't refuse—or at least, I had trouble refusing. The
Army, running short of experienced pilots, decided they would
extend to any pilot in-country the opportunity to stay an extra six
months in Vietnam and at the end of that extension, the pilot could
get out of the Army forever. I thought about this proposal and
wondered, "What would it be like to get on with a normal life?" My
dilemma was: should I take the chance and extend, or go to Fort
Hunter-Stewart and teach non-English-speaking aviators how to fly? I
wrestled with this for an entire day. An additional factor was that my
brother Jon, who had recently gotten married, had just been drafted
and would surely have to come to Vietnam. However, the rule was that
only one sibling had to be in-country at a time. If I stayed, this would

eliminate the possibility of him being in Vietnam as an 11B, an infantryman, whose chances of survival would not be as great as mine, I thought. So there was that. Secondly, I could get on with my life in six months, free of the Army, and go back to college to let "the plan" take its course. I sat down with a calendar, being big into planning and organizing, and figured that if I were to take my next R&R during the Tet Offensive and my seven-day leave during the Spring Offensive, I might miss all the extra-dangerous times of flying.

To enhance the plan, I decided to ask for a transfer to the gunship platoon. I thought that instead of the VC always shooting at me, I would shoot back at them, only with more firepower. An added bonus was that whenever a gunship team went out, it was always as two gunships. This way, I figured, if I *did* get shot down, there would be someone to either cover me or come and pick me up. I marched over to headquarters and told the first sergeant that I wanted to extend for another six months. He looked at me with a bit of dismay and said, "With all that's happened to you in the last twelve months, are you out of your mind?"

"No worries," I said, "I have a plan."

"Well, sir," he answered back, "there's not enough time to get your orders approved before you are due to go home. I don't think it can be done."

"There must be some way this can happen," I pleaded.

Here I was, begging to stay in Vietnam. It should have been a sign from up above to change my mind. He said, "We do have a helicopter going down to Saigon and MACV headquarters tomorrow. Maybe you could hand-carry your request and get it approved. But I still don't think your chances are very good."

"Perfect," I said. "Who's the pilot, and what is the mission?" We had never had a mission that required one of our choppers going all the way down to Saigon. It was at least 600 miles away. The mission was to take the division finance officer down to MACV headquarters. He was a full-bird colonel, so he was pretty important, and the mission must have been priority because he couldn't wait a few days for a C130 to get him there in a quarter of the flight time. I can't remember the name of the assigned A/C for the flight, but after talking to him, it was all arranged that I would ride down to Saigon and, once there, work my way over to MACV headquarters to get the approval I needed.

We left the next morning and made our way from I Corp to III Corp, which was home to MACV and Saigon. Things started to get a little too interesting about an hour into the flight. We were definitely in virgin territory, and the visibility was borderline IFR. It became apparent that we might be getting off course. In other words, lost. I asked if everything was all right, and if I could do anything to help.

"I'm not exactly sure where we are; do you have any ideas?" the A/C asked me.

"Let's land there and ask for directions," I said. I was just as out of my element as he was, but I had spotted a firebase below. It turned out to be a South Korean firebase. Upon landing, I jumped out and walked up to someone in the crowd that was now forming, asking, "Where are we?"

I figured if I knew where we were, then I might have an idea of where to go next. English was definitely not their second language. After a while though, we determined where we were and what our route of flight should be to get back on course. The A/C asked me if I wanted to fly the rest of the trip, and I figured it was worth the risk to get us, and therefore the colonel, there in a timely manner. I shouted to the colonel, "No problems, sir. We're just going to make a scheduled crew change." I'm not sure if he bought it, but all was right when we did, in fact, land at Tan Son Nut Airbase. With the aircraft shut down, the colonel came up to me and said he really appreciated the effort and to let him know if there was anything he could do for me in the future. Little did he know that that request would come just a few days later. Meanwhile, I left the crew. They were going to stay overnight, but they felt confident that there would be no problems on the way home.

"Just keep the ocean on your right and follow it until you come to Chu Lai," I told them. No worries.

Now I had to make my way to MACV headquarters and get my orders approved. I hitched a ride with a young private driving an open-air jeep. We were driving along at a somewhat slow speed because of all the foot traffic, soldiers of the base hustling to and fro. I would imagine with so much brass around they were always under someone's watchful eye. People kept going by our jeep and saluting. After a few minutes I said to the private, "Who are they saluting?"

"I'm pretty sure they are saluting you, sir."

"No shit," I said. "You do that down here?"

"They don't do that where you're from, sir?"

"You do that up north and it could get you killed. The enemy likes to take out officers first."

"Geez, I'd like to be up north," he said.

"Well, it does have its drawbacks," I said, and left it at that.

We arrived at MACV headquarters, and I asked around about where to go, and I was now on the lookout for anyone I had to salute. I never saluted so much in my life as I did that day.

[34]

MUSKETS

THE APPROVAL OF orders was actually painless. No changing my mind now. I was locked and loaded for six more months. I would catch a C130 flight back to Chu Lai the next day, so I had time to kill but no place to stay. Being an officer and in uniform, I was hesitant to do anything that would embarrass myself, Aviation, or the 176th, so my main focus was to find someplace to sleep and stay out of trouble.

Oddly enough, I took a chance hitching another ride, and got lucky that a captain was heading to an area where pretty much all Americans stayed when they were transient. It was late in the day so my plans were to find a hotel and set up for the night. After having heard stories of what could happen in Saigon with random suicide bombers, a possible mugging or two, I was content to stay within the confines of the hotel until the next morning when I was scheduled to leave. From my window, Saigon looked like any other major city I could imagine— crowded streets, vehicle traffic of all modes of transportation, bright lights and noise, soldiers out for a night on the town, Vietnamese looking to make or steal a dollar, and off course MPs. I got a "hop" that was going out to Chu Lai, and in a matter of a few hours I was back at Minuteman Manor.

MY FIRST ORDER of business was to let my parents, siblings, and especially my brother Jon know I wouldn't be coming home as planned. My extension was well thought out, and this would work out best for everyone. Mail being slow, it took many days for the news to reach all interested parties. My parents had actually been waiting for a phone call saying, "Come pick me up." My brother Jon was able to go right to his first sergeant and tell him he couldn't go to Vietnam, his little brother was there. Instead, he was off to Germany, which I was really pleased about.

My next order of business was to talk to CPT Mothersbaugh, the platoon leader for the gunships, about becoming the newest member of the Musket Platoon. Before I made the six-month commitment, I had a preliminary talk with him regarding the plan. I was told I would be flying in a few days with Cop Williams. He was one of the FTLs, or fire team leads, and the most experienced of the gun pilots. He hadn't been in country as long as I had, but he was only a few months short of going home.

I hadn't moved my gear to the Musket hooch yet, that would come in a few days. The slick hooches were at one end of the row and the gunships at the other end. Even though we were all in the same company, there wasn't a great deal of interaction between the two groups, as our flying duties were totally different. As slick drivers, we flew every day with some kind of mission. The gunships usually only went out for combat assaults, medevac recovery, or when the shit was hitting the fan.

There was always a crew that was the primary team. They were on standby, ready to be scrambled at a minute's notice. The secondary team was next up when the primary team was called out. Being next up, secondary had to be ready for anything. A large part of secondary's function was to fill in when the primary team was out but was running low on ammunition or fuel and had to head back. Command would scramble the secondary team so there would be constant coverage for whatever shit they were getting into. On rare occasions, if the first two were out, there would be a third team.

I met Cop at operations for our morning briefing. That morning, we had no inkling what the day's mission was going to be. I knew we had a CA, but it was all kept very hush-hush. We soon found out why. The Americal Division was going to insert a boatload of soldiers into an area just northwest of Tien Fuck. It was a sea of rice paddies that the Viet Cong wanted for themselves. I should have known right then that this didn't sound promising for my first day in gunships.

The area was reported to be an NVA stronghold, with a battalion-sized force that had moved into the area. It was pretty much the same location where I had recently evacuated all the villagers. We were to insert a combined arms force of American troops and South Vietnamese troops into three different locations. The artillery would prep the LZs with 105s and 155s from nearby firebases. The jets would be next in, followed by close air support from our gunships. It was a combined task force of both the 176th and the 71st AHC companies. Just about every available bird was involved in the operation. Cop and I would be the third team into the final LZ. Prior to that, we were just riding cover for the slicks until they went in. We followed the slicks out to their pick-up point, and once the initial load was onboard, we headed out to the first insertion point.

Everything went off without a problem of any kind. No slicks received fire going in or out of the first LZ. Back to the pickup point for more troops, and again out to LZ number two. It was the same— no problem with that drop off either. At that point we were all low on fuel, and the plan was for all aircraft to head back for more fuel and ammo if needed. Once completed, we waited for the final lift of slicks to load up and headed to the last LZ.

Cop and I, with Dan Barrett as our wingman, were the primary team to assist the slicks going into the next LZ. The prep by the artillery and jets was complete, and it was our turn to fly just ahead of the slicks and give one more prep of the area with 2.75 rockets and mini-guns. The command and control aircraft, flying at 1,500 feet with our company commander at the controls, had the brain trust of this operation on board. They could observe and coordinate the entire operation from a safe altitude. The commander had learned from the slick pilots that he could drop smoke from his craft and, if he didn't hit the actual LZ, could give clock directions for inbound aircraft to hit the correct LZ. That way, he could stay above it all, instead of swooping down and perhaps taking fire while marking the LZ.

9—*Gunship patch with my call sign*

The lead gunship usually carried nothing but rockets, while the trail gunship had both rockets and mini-guns to cover lead as he made his turn to come back around for another run at the target. We flew a racetrack pattern, so when the first gunship was breaking off target, the other gunship was just rolling in to cover him and lay down fire. Unlike the Cobra gunships, we also had a crew chief and door gunner. The Cobras could carry more ordnance, but I loved the fact that as we came around from our break, the crew in the back could lay down so much firepower that the enemy couldn't get an easy shot at our blindside like they could with the Cobra.

We started to roll in on target. My job, I thought, was to sit there and learn. I had no assets to fire from my seat, the entire ordnance was controlled by Cop's right seat. I didn't know until that day that, in most cases, a team going in would start their prep at maybe 800–1,000 feet, at 60 knots. When in the correct position, the A/C would roll the nose of the gunship over, picking up speed to quickly hit 120–130 knots. We basically came straight down on target, fired off what ordnance we could and made our turn while the gunners in the back covered our break. As the first gunship would break off their run our wingman would cover the turn. It was a daisy chain of sorts that was repeated until the combat assault was complete.

Easy peasy, I thought. Nobody had taken any fire on the first two insertions, so why should this be any different? Cop started his run. In most cases, gunships would break off at maybe 400–500 feet. Cop must have liked living on the edge. He was (I found out later) notorious for going down to 200–300 feet before he would make his break. He hit the right speed and altitude for firing his 2.75 rockets and squeezed the trigger on his cyclic. Nothing happened, nothing at all.

"What did you do?" he said.

"Nothing," I said. "Was there something I was supposed to do?"

"You were supposed to arm the system."

How was I supposed to know that?

"You never said anything. Give me a hint here, it's my first day on the job."

So, we broke off and got ready to come around again. Meanwhile, nothing in the way of enemy ground fire had happened, so I was sitting fat, dumb, and happy, looking forward to my next on-the-job training moment. We rolled back in, but this time I armed the system. Again I sat back, waiting for the fireworks that were about to begin.

There was one slight problem. The VC on the ground at this LZ must have decided, "If you don't shoot at us, we won't shoot at you." Either that, or they just wanted to wait for the slicks to come in so they could take them all out in one gigantic shoot down. When Cop fired his first pair of rockets, it signaled Charlie that all bets were off, and they started to shoot back. Up until that point, I had taken a lot of ground fire, but never was it like this. We were shooting and they were shooting, only this time they seemed to outnumber us in manpower and firepower. I could tell that they expected us because their weapons were in perfect firing order. They didn't miss a beat.

Thankfully, the crew in the back were working their M-60s just as perfectly. Then it happened. I can only describe it with this little analogy: Imagine driving down the road at a pretty good clip when you come to a very small hill, almost like a bump but not as pronounced. As you go over the bump/hill, you feel like you are coming out of your seat. It's kind of fun when you find one, and you want to go back and do it again. Well, the bump that we felt was an RPG hitting our gunship. It felt like someone had reached down, picked the helicopter up, and then threw it down again, like we hit something in the road, only we were in the air. That happened just as we were making our break.

Within seconds, the door gunner on the right said, "We're on fire!"

I looked back and saw what I thought was just a small fire near the gunner's station. Cop and I were wrestling with the aircraft. At the moment nothing was lit up on the warning panel. I naïvely thought everything was going to be okay, that we would just fly out of this "oh shit" moment.

The VC had a different idea. They didn't let up with the ground fire at all. If anything, they smelled blood and kept pouring it on. It couldn't have been more than a minute later when the door gunner said, "It's getting awfully hot back here." Again I turned around and this time I couldn't even see him. There was a wall of flame between his position and mine.

At a point like that training takes over. To say I was scared would be an understatement. I didn't totally realize what the consequences of that situation could be, but I knew being scared was acceptable, or certainly appropriate as I still had a job to do. Up to then, Cop and I were still flame-free, but we were losing all control of the aircraft. The "engine out" light was on, the hydraulics were failing and now we were starting to spin uncontrollably.

I yelled to the gunner to try and come up front. The crew chief was still pouring whatever 60mm ammo he had left, so I thought for the moment that at least he was okay. We were going down, we had no control over the wounded bird, and the ground was coming up way too fast. This was definitely an "oh fuck" moment.

We actually bounced off some triple canopy jungle, which momentarily brought us upright and level. I had never in my life felt so terrified. I'm sure I was still trying to wrestle the aircraft for bragging rights, but it was past useless. In my attempt to fly the burning hulk, I had seemingly become paralyzed. The last thing I remember was opening my mouth to scream, but nothing seemed to come out.

At that moment, everything became completely quiet and unbelievably calm. I had no awareness of any of the noise that must have been going on around me. I knew Dan Barrett, our wingman, was there and the other two fire teams, who must have been laying down all the firepower they could, but I didn't hear anything. I felt like I was suspended in midair and not inside the burning helicopter. All I could see was a milky white haze around me. There was no definition to the haze. I could reach out to touch and feel it, but there was no end. I was alone, no Cop, no crew, just me. I really didn't care, this was nirvana. *This isn't so bad*, I thought. I liked where I was. I didn't have to be involved with what was going on down below me. I could see everything that had happened to 333, the tail number of our aircraft. I saw its burning mass, crumbled into a rice paddy, nose down left.

Then reality set in. The next thing I knew, I could see my body down in that destroyed helicopter, calling me to come down. I thought, "No way, I'm staying right here. It's incredibly peaceful and calm up here! Why would I want to go back to a burning helicopter?"

I was overruled by the aviation gods. The next memory I have is of Cop pulling on me, shaking me to either see if I was alive or else to drag my body out of the chopper. I suddenly came to. The part of me—my spirit perhaps—that was watching everything below had joined my body again. It took a few seconds to realize I was still alive, and a millisecond to realize we were still on fire.

Cop climbed up and out to his side of the aircraft, where for some reason, he seemed to hesitate. *This is no time to be afraid of heights*," I thought, and pushed him out the jettisoned door with me right behind him. The fall was only a few feet as the chopper was half buried in the rice paddy. Once outside, we heard the gunner, Rick, screaming for help. He was still trapped in the gunner's position. Both of us waddled back to him.

We reached Rick, and Cop started trying to pull him free. Everything seemed to be happening in slow motion. In almost a comedy of errors, I looked at Cop and said, "He still has his seatbelt harness on." Cop looked at me with a what-are-we-going-to-do look, and I grabbed the gunner's survival knife and started cutting Rick loose from the harness. His leg looked as though it was partially pinned by the aircraft. Once he was free from the harness, I was trying to push what was left of the helicopter off of him.

We finally got him out and dragged him over to a rice dike for some protection. At that point, I was thinking, "Okay, the war is over for me. I'm just going to stay here and hide until there is a declared truce. I've got rice that will last me forever, the scenery is lush, and I don't have to fly anymore."

That's when Cop said to me, "Where's Don?" Don was the crew chief on the left side.

"I don't know."

He gave me a look and said, "Why don't you go and see?" I was aware of the fact that in the gunship platoon I was the new guy, and because of that, he outranked me in the helicopter, but on the ground I was the ranking officer. I was thinking, "Shouldn't I stay here, and you go look?"

This was no time for discussion though, so I half low-crawled, half waddled to the left side of the burning helicopter. I got as close as I could and peered inside. I didn't see a body. I could hear bullets cracking all around me and knew the enemy was close to nailing my butt for good. Water droplets from the rice paddy were spitting up at me from the AK-47s, so I decided to run through the helicopter to see if I could feel for Don's body. I got to the other side, but I didn't feel a corpse, so I waddled back to the edge of the rice dike.

"He's not there," I said.

For some reason, when we all got out of the gunship, Cop took off his chicken plate but kept his helmet on. I, on the other hand, decided to keep my chicken plate on. It had worked for me before, so I was going with it again. In addition, because of an almost-deadly incident with a crew chief and a loaded weapon aimed at me, I never carried my .38 pistol loaded. Now I was trying to load my pistol, but I was just jamming mud, rice, and bullets into the chamber, and I knew that wasn't going to work. I finally got so frustrated that I threw my weapon toward the enemy, hoping to hit them in the head or else thinking, "You try and load this thing." (After that, I carried the much heavier Colt .45, which had two safeties but was always loaded.) Dan Barrett, God love him, believed in "Leave no man behind." That, or he was just coming down to count and/or collect the bodies. He started to land. A gunship is not designed to carry a lot of people. It is usually weighted down with ammo, rocket pods, and machine guns. Yet down he came, and with another ship right behind him.

Just as they touched down, I saw what I thought was a VC running out of the jungle, heading straight for the second landing helicopter. All I could think was that it was an enemy running to blow himself up in that helicopter. So I grabbed Cop and Rick and ran as fast as possible, given the circumstances, toward Dan and dove into his helicopter. They pulled pitch immediately, and I crawled into the tiniest little ball imaginable. I was going to make myself so small I would be invisible.

Dan still had to climb the overweight gunship out of the area. It seemed to take days to be finally clear of the danger zone. When we reached 1,000 feet, I thought maybe I had made it and was relieved to be alive. Everyone on board was elated, none of us could believe that we were safe. I was working on Cop and Rick's wounds, as much as anything to keep myself distracted from what had just happened while trying to ignore the burning sensation coming from my face. I yelled to the gunner of the rescue bird, "Does my face look okay? Because something doesn't feel right."

He said, "Oh yeah, you look fine."

I could see that the clothes on my left side were burned off, but I still had my arm. My thoughts turned to our crew chief. I assumed that he had died in the crash. I felt responsible that I hadn't been able to find him, let alone save him. I felt guilty that I was alive and he was probably dead.

It wasn't until later at the hospital that I found out the VC that I thought I saw running for the other helicopter wasn't a VC at all, it was our crew chief, Don. It had gotten so hot in the back of Triple-Three (333) that he decided to take his chances jumping from the spinning helicopter from maybe a hundred feet. He landed in some triple canopy jungle and bounced his way down. He ended up with maybe twenty stitches in his knee and that was all. The entire incident can only be described as a miracle.

We were heading for the hospital. *Things would be okay now*, I thought. Once inside, the staff was cutting off what was left of my clothes. I was trying to stifle a few groans so I didn't come off like a big baby, but damn, it hurt. The three of us were separated, assigned to individual doctors. They gave me a shot of something, and the next thing I knew life was good. I wasn't feeling much of anything anymore.

I woke up in a ward, lying next to Rick. I was told by a nurse not to move if I could help it. Easier said than done. Seventy-five percent of my face was burned, along with the left side of my body, which was a combination of bandages and burned flesh. Lying on my back was to be my comfortable position while trying not to move. There was one problem. In a gunship, just behind the pilot's seat was a netting to keep the spent M-60 casings from coming forward. This netting, however, had burned in the fire, and one of the hot shell casings somehow managed to hit the back of my helmet, go down my shirt, and burn the bejesus out of me. I couldn't be more uncomfortable. I didn't want to sound like a baby, but my face was still hurting like hell. I would ask everyone that came up to me, "Does my face look all right?"

The answer was always, "Oh yeah, sure."

That first night was a series of catnaps, waiting for another day. The next afternoon, my platoon leader, CPT Mothersbaugh, came to see me and said, "If you feel as bad as you look, you must feel like shit."

I said, "That's it. Somebody get me a mirror." What I saw was what had to be my face, but one with no eyebrows, not much hair on the top of my head, ears sticking completely perpendicular to my head, blisters the size of golf balls, and dead or burnt skin hanging down.

Holy shit, I thought.

FOLLOWING A FEW days of hospitalization, the Division Finance officer would visit wounded soldiers in order to have all the paperwork ready for when they were to be shipped home. This was the same colonel I had helped get to Saigon. He looked at me, looked at the name on the chart, looked at me again, then my chart again, and finally said, "Are you the pilot that got me to Saigon?"

"Yes, sir."

"What the hell happened to you?"

I explained in very short detail what had happened, and he asked what he could do for me. There were two things I wanted—or badly needed—from him. First, when we were wounded, someone usually notified our next-of-kin, which in my case would be my parents. This couldn't happen because for the entire time I had been in Vietnam, they thought I was not flying any combat missions, that I was strictly a maintenance pilot. Plus, they didn't even know at this point that I wasn't coming home as scheduled. The slow pace mail meant they wouldn't know of my extension for a few more days. I didn't want someone to notify them and say, "Your son is not coming home as planned," and, "Oh by the way, your son has been shot down and he's in the hospital."

The second and more important fact was that soldiers with wounds that needed more extensive medical attention were usually

155

sent home to the U.S. I couldn't have that. I had just extended for six months to get out of the Army early. I wasn't going to have gone through all this just to be sent home and still be in the Army for another two and a half years. He told me he would do what he could, but there were no guarantees. I thanked him and said anything he could do would be helpful.

My first order of business in my recovery was to let someone in the family know that I had been through a shoot-down. A very nice nurse took a little dictation for a letter to my younger brother, Mark. I thought that if the colonel couldn't prevent the Army from notifying my parents, I wanted a family member to able to say to them, "I've heard from Wayne, and he's going to be all right." If I communicated with them directly, they would know I was not just a pilot flying maintenance and would start to worry all over again. Later on, Mark told me that the day he got the letter, he had a scheduled exam at college and using me as an excuse he went running to the professor and said he was too distraught to take the exam. I'm not sure if he was given a pass on the exam or not.

Rick and I had physical therapy to do. We were told that if we could walk, then we should be up and about to prevent scarring. This could be accomplished by various physical therapy measures. There was nothing wrong with my legs, so I would push Don up and down the ward in a wheelchair to keep stretching the skin.

We learned from some of the guys who came to visit us that when the ground troops from all three insertions had completed the operation, they found that the area was not Viet Cong-controlled, it was a battalion-sized force of NVA, or North Vietnamese Army. They had captured stores of rice and ammo. They even discovered a twenty-man hospital dug into the side of a mountain. It was a huge blow to the NVA.

Believe it or not, there was television on the ward floor It had one channel from Armed Forces Network, or something like that. If I paid attention, I could pick up a little of the Vietnamese language on the only channel, usually once a day. I was okay with what I knew already: "I love you," "How much money," etc.—the basics. The television

156

also had sporting events that were happening back home. There was one slight problem. They would show the event three times within a 24-hour period, and it was always on a tape-delay. That way, soldiers who had guard duty or a late shift could catch the game later on. It became a little tiresome to watch an event three times in one day when I already knew the final score of the game a week earlier from the *Stars and Stripes* newspaper. On the plus side, after one viewing, Rick and I decided time was better spent doing our physical therapy. We spent two weeks at that hospital before they decided Don was going home and I was to be transferred to another hospital. The colonel must have pulled some strings, because I was getting to stay in Vietnam. Gee, how lucky was I? I got what I wanted, I guess.

AT THAT FIRST hospital, I was able to see some of the guys—Fast Eddy, Steve, and Dave Young—as often as possible. At the smaller hospital, I lost all communication with my fellow pilots from the 176th. they were still flying every day, and it was a tougher location for them to get to.

The doctors at my new location wanted to try a different kind of treatment on me, a new burn medicine that the other hospital wasn't aware of, and which they thought might have better results. I spent another two weeks at this hospital until the staff came to a decision. I was to go home for two weeks or so and check in with the local VA to see how I was progressing.

It had the makings of a "good news, bad news" scenario. It was just one week before Christmas, and it would be nice to see the family. The bad news was, how was I going to explain why my face looked the way it did? I would worry about that later. I was getting out of the hospital and that was good by me. I thanked the staff for all they had done and headed back to Minuteman Manor.

A side note: when I first got to the hospital, the staff had to cut off my clothes to tend to my wounds but my combat flying boots had zippers to be able to get them on and off in a hurry. I assumed they had just unzipped my boots and I could collect them later, but they cut those off as well. "Didn't you see the zippers?" I asked. They gave me a look like, "You ungrateful asshole." Really, I liked those boots!

[35]

DEATH BECOMES REAL

ONCE BACK AT the Manor, I started making preparations to go home. It was December 15, and the battalion commander had called a very rare meeting for all the 176th that night. He wanted to thank us for the job we had been doing up to this point. The weather was miserable, as it was the end of the monsoon season, and we were sitting under low ceilings in heavy rain. He made a point of saying nobody would be flying that night and if they did, it would have to be approved by him personally.

That was a relief to Dee Hyden, as he was on the flare mission. Dee hated flying at night. It didn't happen that often, but when your number came up for flare duty, you did your job. Dee was from Amarillo, Texas, and had the biggest smile on his face all the time. He had red hair, so the smile always stood out. He would have stood out in any crowd he might have been in.

We were sitting on top of our bunker when the call to scramble came in. You could almost see the terror in his eyes. You knew when the call came someone out there needed help that only a flight crew could bring. I'm not sure what time at night it was, but the call came through to scramble the flare ship for a medevac mission, and it was approved, After all, it was a medevac mission, and that usually trumped all sound reasoning that said it might be too dangerous. Dee's crew ran out to the aircraft, as well as the gunship crew that would be covering the medevac bird.

Normally, a flare ship had a crew of five on board: aircraft commander, a peter pilot, the crew chief, gunner, and an extra crew chief to help with dropping the flares. Two crew chiefs, Larry Keeler and Don Rose, were leaving to go home the next day and decided to do one more run for old time's sake. They kicked the scheduled crew chief and gunner off and said they would take over.

Dee took off from Minuteman Manor and at the end of our strip made a right turn to head towards the LZ. They weren't more than 500 feet off the ground when they went inadvertent IMC, a weather condition that is in the clouds and flying ability is then strictly by instruments. If you're prepared for it, you can make adjustments. Inadvertent means it totally took you by surprise and only in the best conditions could you manage. We'll never know, but it was thought that Dee decided to have the crew drop a flare to help him see better. Dee must have gotten completely disoriented and suffered vertigo. The body tells us what it thinks it's feeling, but our brain has to fight through that feeling and trust the instruments. Once in the grasps of vertigo, it's very hard to get out of it.

The gunships that were behind him watched him go upside-down and crash just a hundred yards off the end of our area. The helicopter exploded on impact, all souls were lost, and due to the quantity of flares on board, it burned for hours. Don Stockton, a lieutenant, and Bill Barritt were the other crewmembers with Dee. Steve Kerchenfaunt, a great guy from Ohio and someone I flew with a lot, had been working in operations that night. I had taken to mentoring Steve on all that I had learned, and we got along very well. He came to my room, visibly shaken and told me what had happened. My constant thought was, *No, that can't be. The commander said no one would be flying tonight.* We just sat there shaking our heads, not believing five family members had just died and two of them had not even belonged on the aircraft in the first place.

Up to this point we had lost several 176th personnel to death or wounds that sent them home. This night was deeper for me. The previous deaths of Bruce Macalister and his crew of Butler, Ford, and Bailey had been a grim reminder of what may lie ahead. It was personal then but Dee's death and that of his crew was especially hard. I liked Dee, everyone did. I sat there thinking of his last moments, hoping that seconds before his death he found the same nirvana that I had. I didn't want to lose him but I didn't want him to suffer. Five soldiers that I would see on a daily basis, five soldiers that ate what I ate, five soldiers that maybe had the same dreams and hopes for the future, five soldiers bound for graves registration who wouldn't be going home alive.

It was ten days before Christmas, and it hit all of us in the company very hard. Each time we departed or approached Minuteman Manor we would fly right over what was left of the wreckage. It was a bleak reminder every day.

[36]

GOING HOME

I ARRIVED AT Seattle-Tacoma airport, December 22, 1969. I had to fend for myself for reservations to get back to Boston, no easy task just before Christmas. I was moved from one standby flight to another, and I thought for a while that I might be spending Christmas in the Seattle-Tacoma airport. I was bored out of my mind and even shaved three times just for something to do (at that age I really didn't need to shave at all). Finally, there was a break, and on Christmas Eve I was on a flight to Boston. I had come up with what I thought was an ingenious story to explain the burns on my face and arm. Most of my hair and eyebrows had started to grow back to a passable length, and I thought just maybe they would pass the "Mom test."

Remember, I had told my parents that I was a maintenance pilot, never flying in combat situations. How was I to explain the scars? My intention was to not have my parents worrying about me while in-country. Why would anyone want to put their loved ones through that daily anguish? What was the point of something I couldn't control and something they couldn't control? It just seemed to be the way to go. I never shared the loss of life with them, they may have thought I might be next. I thought my dad would be a piece of cake. Upon landing, though, I was a nervous wreck. In minutes, I would be facing my parents, hoping they would buy my story about my face.

Intentionally, I was one of the last passengers off the plane. I'm sure it drove my parents crazy waiting for me, but I was more afraid of their reaction than I cared to admit. We came face to face and my dad immediately said, "What the hell happened to your face?"

"Jeez, Dad, I thought Mom would be the one to notice first."

My mom shot my dad the "look" and replied, "I saw it right away, but I didn't want to scare the poor boy."

Okay, that went well. Then, just like I planned, I told them my story: "We had a going-away party for a couple of the pilots, and there was heavy drinking. Being the lightweight that I am, I passed out in my bunk while smoking. The mattress caught fire and I got burned." Did they believe me? They did. I passed the test. It was a genuinely fun ride home. Once on the Cape, I settled into family, food, and a few beers. My sister Ellen and her husband came up from Connecticut. Mark was home from school, but Jon was stationed in Germany with his wife, Joyce.

I was walking down the hallway of our new house when Ellen caught up to me and pressed. "What happened to your face? It did not happen while you were smoking in bed." I thought I could try to deny, deny, deny, but I knew she had me. I pulled her into the bathroom and told her the story and told her not to let Mom and Dad know.

"They don't think I'm doing that much flying over there," I told her. "I did tell Mark, so if the Army notified our parents, Mark could say everything was going to be all right." She accepted my response and said she wouldn't say anything, but she pleaded with me to be careful over there. I told her that all the bad things that could happen to me already had, and that I had a plan.

The army had a plan for me too. The VA doctors in Boston said my healing was on track, so I could return to Vietnam.

[37]

GOING BACK

BRUCE RIDDLE (MUFF) was home on leave in Los Altos, California, because his mother had recently passed. He wasn't scheduled to go back until later. I made arrangements to go to his house and hang out for a few days before my flight back to 'Nam. We had a grand time, as short as it was. He had a flight attendant girlfriend, and she had a friend. Muff must have prepped her because she was very nice to me. Maybe she felt she had some kind of patriotic duty.

I wish they'd had frequent flyer miles back then, I would have made a score, or at the very least I would have been upgraded at every opportunity. I landed in Cam Ranh Bay, and this time I was prepared for the smell. I think I remember saying to nobody in particular, "Welcome to Vietnam," as some newbies came to a stop at the door. I was no longer the new guy. Now I was the old guy.

From Cam Ranh Bay I got on a C130 to Chu Lai, took a jeep ride, and there I was, back at Minuteman Manor. Going home to the Cape now seemed like a distant memory for me. You could hardly call my time home as a vacation. It was more of a relief to be absent from people shooting at you.

In the beginning, my time away from Vietnam seemed to have an air of infinity to it. *Did I really have to go back? Couldn't I just stay here and be done with the war?*

Returning to Chu Lai had an odd feel to it. I was back in the danger zone. I knew better the environment, the sights, the smell, and the danger—my learning curve was seemingly complete. Still, it was great to catch up with the pilots who were still there. Fast Eddy was going to be in the gunship platoon, as well as Dave Young. Dave was from Missouri and been in-country about six months. Like the rest of us he was lean but hardly mean. Quiet, slightly soft spoken yet a professional at the tender age of twenty-one. Steve Kerchenfaunt my protege was now an aircraft commander in the second platoon, and his call sign was Minuteman two-three. I was extremely happy with that, as I felt our call sign was our legacy and there was none better than Steve to carry on the tradition.

[38]

MUSKET THREE-TWO

IT DIDN'T TAKE long to get up to speed with flying in the gunship platoon. Obviously the tactics were different, but a Huey is a Huey. On my first flight after coming back, I was paired with Paul Lent. Paul was a big guy, quick with a smile and laid back. We were the lead fire team for a combat assault into an area just south of My Lai. Though it was only my second flight in guns, I was sure it couldn't be as bad as my first. Once again I was sitting left-seat on the lead bird, so no toys for me, though I did remember to arm the rocket system before we made our run. Paul started his run, and I was just watching how it was done.

We started at about 1,000 feet, just ahead of the slicks that were dropping off their troops. We picked up speed quickly and Paul went to fire the first set of rockets to prep the LZ. On my side of the aircraft the rocket pods were just about abeam of my door. As the rockets came out of the tubes they made a whooshing sound and we could almost feel the helicopter wanting to jerk back from the thrust of the rockets. All of a sudden there was a problem. As the rocket on the left side got halfway out of the tube, it stuck, yet the rocket motor was still firing away, spitting propellant out in all directions.

This is my second day for God's sake! I thought. *What is going on?* There I sat, about three feet from this rocket that was going haywire in the tube. I thought the rocket was going to blow up and finally end my misery. I had no idea if this could even happen, so the Irish Catholic in me assumed the worst. Paul broke off the run when he realized what had happened and "trail-rolled" in, laying down his rockets and miniguns. We continued to fly the racetrack pattern, covering the trail aircraft with the gunner's M-60. He kept trying to tell me that it should be okay, but I was not feeling as good about it as he was.

So after trail had laid down its entire ordnance and the troops were safely on the ground, Paul headed out over the Pacific Ocean just a few miles from our present position. Once over the water, he jettisoned the rocket pod. Landing with a live rocket at Minuteman Manor was out of the question. When we landed at the Manor, we refitted a new pod and got ready to head back out to the LZ in case the ground troops ran into trouble. I was really having my doubts about switching to gunships. Two flights, two mishaps—was it going to get better?

IT DID GET better. After a while I was made a fire team lead. Fast Eddy Covill, Dave Young (who had joined the Musket platoon), and I would hold court every night, with Ed always sucking on an unfiltered Pall Mall. The bonds were the same—unbreakable—and we were there for each other. My call sign would be Musket three-two, I just flipped the two with the three. It seemed a perfect fit.

Inexplicably, my "magnet ass" reputation waned a bit. Maybe it was payback in a good way, or maybe the VC knew we had a whole lot more firepower to shoot back with now. No more approaches in and exits out of an LZ with Charlie lining us up for the kill. On the other hand, when we did get scrambled, it meant something was happening and there would inevitably be groundfire. In addition, there were always two gunships. I already knew firsthand that trail would do whatever was possible to cover us or get us out of harm's way, so I took my chances with being able to fight back.

As I already mentioned, the lead gunship usually had nothing but rockets, along with two door gunners to lay down additional firepower and cover us on the break. The trail gunship had both rockets and mini-guns—not as many rockets, but enough to do some damage. The mini-gun, on the other hand, could lay down a volume of fire, if necessary, that could put a bullet in every square foot of a football field in sixty seconds—approximately 3,000-4,000 rounds a minute. I never wanted to be anywhere that I had to lay down that much lead. Inevitably that would be a bad situation. Both aircraft had a rocket-sight that we could flip down for improved accuracy, but we also drew a grease-pen marking on the windshield. This way we could roll the helicopter nose over, line the grease mark up with the target, and fire with pretty decent accuracy.

On one occasion we were covering a slick insertion into an area near a small village south of LZ Stinson. We rolled in to provide cover, and the villagers must have known we were coming because they decided to *didi mau* as quickly as they could. The Viet Cong were in the village as well, and to mask their escape they herded a bunch of the villagers down a road leading out of the village.They looked like a swarm of ants clustered together and scurrying down the road.

The command and control ship (C&C) called on me to stop those people. My run was perpendicular to the road, so I didn't have much to line up on for the run. I only had my grease-pencil mark to take the shot. I rolled over, trying to come down as vertical as I could to make the most of the two rockets. A shallow approach run could mean the rockets I was about to squeeze off might land too short or too long. Neither scenario was going to stop the mass exodus from the village. In most cases, a pair of rockets didn't have to hit the target squarely to get a good killing field. It was kind of like horseshoes—close was good enough. I had hoped that the impact would be far enough from the fleeing villagers but close enough to make them rethink their departure. I squeezed the cyclic trigger, firing off a pair of rockets, and damn if I didn't hit dead-center on the road, just in front of the villagers heading out of Dodge. You have to visualize what a swarm of ants running in mass looks like when the road blows up not more than seventy-five yards in front of them. They did an immediate about face and headed at full speed back to the village, Viet Cong be damned. It was far and away the luckiest shot I ever had with any pair of rockets I fired. Even the C&C ship came over the radio saying, "Nice shot, you lucky bastard."

It was kind of a running joke for a few days that the only thing I could hit was a road. It did the job, however, which was to keep the villagers in the village until the ground troops could move in. Of course, after my break we started to take some fairly heavy ground fire. I'm not sure if my accuracy was as good then, as the enemy were hidden in a tree line and I could only guess whether I was hitting anything.

THERE WAS ANOTHER village that both Fast Eddy and I, as a fire team, would be remembered by. A small village near My Lai had come under attack and the CAP team that was embedded in the village called for help. We scrambled to the location and were given range and azimuth or direction to the enemy. We placed all our firepower on several runs, and the enemy broke contact. This wasn't necessarily significant to us, but it must have been to the people of the village because, days later, Ed and I were told to report with our respective crews from that day to an area located inside Minuteman Manor's perimeter. We all thought this was odd but did as we were told.

Some of the locals from that village, along with some members of the CAP team, had prepared a banquet for us. Slightly embarrassed, we sat down to a Vietnamese feast. We had fish (which would probably be called sushi today), rice, rice bread, rice wine, and warm cans of Pepsi. I've always been a meat and potatoes man. Even with my Catholic upbringing, Fridays meant peanut butter sandwiches or spaghetti, no sauce. I'd never had fish of any kind, and up to that point I don't think I'd had rice. Those who know me know what I like, and I don't tend to stray too far from that, but I wanted to be polite, eating the rice and drinking the warm Pepsi. I have never had white rice or warm Pepsi since, although I did finally acquire a slight taste for fish.

[39]

R&R

REMEMBER THAT PLAN I had made before extending for six months? As so often happens, the best-laid plans of mice and men went awry that very first day. The only part of the plan that was still on track was a seven-day leave during the Tet Offensive "holidays." It was during this period that the NVA and Viet Cong tried to wreak as much havoc as they could to remind the local populace who was actually in charge. Tet was here, but my orders for a seven-day leave were in hand.

Seven-day leaves went by seniority. Those who had been in-country the longest got priority—first in, first out—to the paradise of their choosing. The NCOs gathered everyone in a group and started calling out the places we could choose from. Hong Kong was the first location offered. I had been wanting to go there for a while, especially after hearing stories from others who had come back with quite an array of electronics, cameras, and tailor-made clothes. Australia was for the birds. I couldn't wait for Hong Kong.

The NCOs would state a date and say, "If anyone has been in-country prior to this date and wants to go to Hong Kong, step forward." The date he called out seemed prior to the invention of the automobile, and everybody laughed. Who would be crazy enough to have been here that long? The next date was called, and a gaggle of soldiers were still laughing when I stepped forward. A hush came over the crowd, and I got looks that said, "Oh yeah, that's the dude with two combat patches." That was okay by me. I was going to Hong Kong and they weren't. *Who's laughing now?*

I landed in Hong Kong amid a sea of people. It was so crowded, and yet there was an exciting energy about it. Hotel space was very scarce. I was forced to share a room with someone else, which I thought was rather odd, but what was I to do? By chance, Don Alexander, a fellow pilot from the 176th, had also made the trip to Hong Kong on a scheduled R&R. We ended up sharing a room in one of Hong Kong's finest hotels. After sleeping on a thirty-inch bunk for fourteen months or so, anything would have seemed five-star.

We had similar ideas of what we wanted to do in Hong Kong, and women of ill-repute were not on top of the list. In the lobby of our hotel, we met an Australian who said he'd always wanted to see Hong Kong, and we wound up hitting it off. We ventured out into the Kowloon district for a night of cruising and looking at all the city had to offer. We were committed to just walking around and being good. My first impression of the city was the number of people walking the streets. It seemed like a sea of people moving like a tide. People-watching was an attraction in and of itself. Obviously, there were native Chinese and Americans, but in addition perhaps every nationality was represented. The neon lights of the city seemed to make the night as bright as the day. From the small hamlets of Vietnam to the streets of Hong Kong was such a complete contrast it almost boggled the mind. It was a welcomed change just to be part of this world.

We had been walking for maybe an hour or so, taking it all in, when we happened by a bar that had women standing outside inviting us to come in and buy them a "Hong Kong tea." Hong Kong tea was nothing but ginger ale for a mere fifteen dollars—a pretty steep price back in 1970. "No thank you, ladies," we told them, "We are just out for a walk." They were persuasive, but we stuck to our guns and kept walking.

The plan, in its intent, was good. Our knowledge of Hong Kong geography was not. We were walking down a dead-end street and didn't know it. We reached the end of the street, and we knew we would have to walk past the women on our return. The temptation the second time was too great, and we caved. It had been six months since I had been with a woman. Not sure if it was feeling like a civilian without my uniform on, the loneliness, or just being plain horny. It was easily excusable to give in. I have always found Asian women to be attractive but in their profession good looks wasn't a key requirement. To these women I probably represented dollar signs. Their approach was next girl up.

After much money wasted on ginger ale, Don and I left the brothel with two of Hong Kong's finest. We headed back to our hotel but strict moral codes forced us to bring the girls into the hotel by way of the service elevator. It seemed odd to Don and me but these professionals knew all the ins and outs of the access to the hotel. We were at their mercy. We had hit a point of no return so there was no squabbling about a dollar amount. We were easy pickings if you know what I mean, and I think you do. It goes without saying that after a very short time we said goodbye to Hong Kong's finest. They asked us to come by the next night as well, eager to make another quick score. When we woke up the next day, substantially poorer, we vowed that that was going to be our only indiscretion this vacation.

That morning, Don and I went our separate ways but planned to meet up later in the day. My first stop was to the garment district to find a tailor. Even with his limited English skills, he understood what I wanted. I had pictures from a magazine and showed him how it should look. "No problem," he said, taking measurements and telling me to come back in two days. I then went hunting for top-of-the-line stereo equipment. The choices were endless, and I ended up with some primo equipment. I was going to have a great sound system for back in the real world. I met Don at the hotel, and we promised each other not to visit any brothels that night. We met up with our Australian friend and went out again for drinks at a little bar that had a dance floor, which we thought would be fun to just watch from afar. The bar was called the Yellow Submarine, aptly named since it was down a flight of stairs. It had a pretty good crowd but was not overcrowded.

A waitress came up and took our order—and besides my order, she also took my breath away. She was an incredibly beautiful French Chinese girl, maybe French Polynesian, with dark hair, beautiful skin, and a gorgeous smile. Not overly petite but small with an incredible figure. By any standards, she was drop-dead beautiful. When she came back with the drinks, I couldn't help but stare at her. I thanked her, and, in perfect English, she replied, "You're welcome."

Don was not shy with women, and he talked to anyone who would listen. I sat there by myself just watching the crowd and nursing a beer. After a while, the same beautiful waitress came up and asked if I would like another beer.

"Sure, I guess," I said.

Things at the Yellow Submarine started to slow down, and the crowd thinned out. This presented an awkward moment or two of me inadvertently staring at this girl. Don moved from girl to girl, talking about being a helicopter pilot in Vietnam. He wasn't bashful.

"You should talk to some of the girls here," he told me. "They're not at all like last night's duo."

"Nah," I said. "I'm good. Don't worry about me. I'm having a good time, really."

A few beers and I was off to the men's room. With real running water and no rats, it was a luxury. When I came back, Don interrupted his conversation with girl number three to say, "Our waitress followed you with her eyes all the way to the bathroom and back."

"You're crazy."

"Seriously, she watched you the whole way. Ask my friend here, she saw it too." The girl shook her head in agreement. *Hot damn*, I thought, and that's as far as I thought. It was probably the empty beer glass that brought the waitress back to the table, but when she came, the girl Don had been talking to said something to her in Chinese. She looked at me with what seemed an embarrassed look and smiled. *Great*, I thought, *Now what?* With that, she asked me if I wanted to dance. I was stunned.

Don was pushing me from the table and off I went. Her name was Mei Ling. It meant a delicate and beautiful plum, or something like that. She told me that if business was a little slow, and it didn't interfere with her primary job of serving drinks, she could dance with the customers, and that if it was a little busy, she could still dance but the customer would have to talk to her boss and pay a fee to dance with a waitress so that he didn't lose money. I was willing to pay whatever amount he wanted just to talk to her. The night ended, and Don and I headed back to the hotel, but not before I said I would be back the next night.

The next night it was the same scenario: a few beers, a dance or two, and some great conversation. She wanted to travel and see the world by way of being an airline flight attendant. She could escape the daily grind of Hong Kong life and travel to faraway lands. We talked of my love for flying and I told her she would absolutely feel the same. We rambled on while we had the chance. The night ended far too quickly, only this time she asked me if I would like to explore more of Hong Kong the next morning. I responded with an emphatic yes but mentioned that I had to go to the tailor's for a quick fitting. No problem, she said, she would meet me outside the hotel and we could go together.

We did just that, and she had some helpful suggestions about what might look good on me. The tailor told me to come back in two days and everything would be ready. With that, Mei Ling and I had the rest of the afternoon to ourselves. We walked all over Hong Kong. While it wasn't very large geographically, it was very crowded. Then we took a ferry to Hong Kong Island, took a tram up Victoria's Peak, and just wandered around talking. Victoria's Peak is a hill on the western half of Hong Kong Island. It is also known as Mount Austin, and locally as The Peak. With an elevation of about 1,550 feet you had a panoramic view of the bustling city below. Your senses had trouble trying to fathom how such a small parcel of land could hold so many people. From this vantage point it was a beautiful city that masked the hustle and bustle.

I won't go into details but suffice it to say, we ended up back at the hotel and spent two unbelievable days together. My seven-day leave came to an end far too quickly, but it was time to head back to Vietnam. Mei Ling helped me pick up my clothes and sent some of them to the U.S. The rest of the things I took back to Vietnam with me. I said my goodbyes to Mei Ling and had visions of jumping on a steamer in Seattle and coming back to find her, maybe spending the rest of my life there. Mei Ling consumed my mind the entire return trip to Vietnam. I couldn't stop thinking about what she did for my mind and body. I was determined to figure out how I could make it back to Hong Kong, fly for an airline, and have her on board as one of the flight attendants. I was a sucker for love, and a plus was that I didn't bring back anything unwanted, as I had from Australia.

[40]

LIGHT AT THE END OF

THE TUNNEL

I ARRIVED BACK at the Manor, relieved to learn that the 176th had been relatively quiet for the rest of the Tet Offensive. Mostly it was the usual—CAs (combat assaults), ground units in trouble, and medevac. A new twist that was a bit boring was flying cover for the CH-54 heavy-lift helicopters, which were relatively new to our area but needed gunship coverage every time they went out on a mission. Their flight profile was always a sling-load mission at a hundred-foot hover, which made them very inviting targets. For us, this meant flying a high circle around them in case the NVA or VC wanted to take a shot.

On a day that Eddy and I were scheduled off, both primary and secondary teams had been scrambled, which left the two of us to be the third team up. It was rare that a third team would be called up, but sure enough, the bat-phone rang in the hooch to scramble a fire team for a unit in contact. Without putting much thought into it, Eddy and I ran with another crew to launch two aircrafts. By this I mean that we ran out to the aircraft with the bare minimum of flight equipment. I didn't have my chicken plate, and Eddy thought his helmet was in the aircraft, which wasn't the case, but we didn't have time to run back and get our proper gear. We cranked in minutes and headed out to the location of contact.

Since Eddy didn't have a helmet, we were yelling back and forth about what we were going to do. I called the ground unit, and they gave us range and azimuth to the enemy. We started our runs—Eddy on mini-guns, me on rockets. We rained down "Musket havoc" on the enemy, and they broke contact.

Once back at the Manor, we looked at each other and both thought, *How dumb was that to not have our proper gear?* If the VC had only known, they might have prolonged the party just to teach us a lesson. Eddy held court again that night, and all the other pilots got a kick out of our day's escapade.

I WAS COMING up on 1,500 hours of combat time, which I was told later was a pretty high mark not only for our company but also for a majority of the aviation companies in Vietnam. I didn't care much, a number's just a number.

The spring offensive was fast approaching, coinciding with my scheduled R&R to Bangkok. I had planned for R&R to be three weeks prior to my long-awaited return to the real world. I would have gone back to Hong Kong to see Mei Ling but the arrangements had been made back in November and couldn't be changed. I was sad I would not get to sit and stare into her gorgeous face and a little angry at myself. I rationalized this struggle with the fact Bangkok would be a place I might otherwise never get a chance to see.

I had just finished flying a mission and had shut the aircraft down when Captain Andy Johnson came up to my aircraft. I was still sitting in my seat when he said, "I've got good news and bad news. Which do you want first?"

"Give me the bad news first," I said.

"You're not going to Bangkok."

"What, how can that be? It's already set up—they can't do that."

"Do you want the good news?" he asked.

"Well it had better be pretty spectacular," I replied.

He said with a huge grin on his face, "You got a twenty-day drop. You're going home."

"Oh my God, are you serious? Or is this a joke? Because it won't be funny."

He was serious. I was leaving Vietnam in two days. To say I was excited would be an understatement. Bangkok would wait for another time, I was going home. The best part about it was that I didn't have to do upcoming missions wondering if something would go fatally wrong with just weeks to go.

I walked back to my hooch with a big grin on my face. My Musket teammates already knew. I had just enough time to pack my gear and say my goodbyes. I got the news on a Tuesday and would be leaving Thursday. Tuesday night we celebrated. I took a lot of pictures with the new camera I had gotten in Hong Kong, memories courtesy of Nikon. I snapped away and finished one roll, starting in on roll number two. The problem was that in taking the roll of film out and putting a new one in, I exposed all the pictures I had taken and didn't know it. I could fly a helicopter, but I couldn't change a roll of film. Go figure.

Tuesday night I went to bed thinking of what Thursday would bring. There was a part of me that was excited and relieved to be going home, but there was also part of me that felt I was abandoning my fellow aviators. Why couldn't we just all go home together? I ran the gamut between ecstasy and guilt. I was not the first to experience these feelings, and I was sure I wouldn't be the last.

That very night we took incoming rockets and mortars. It took us by surprise for maybe ten seconds. When the first round hit, the natural reaction was, "What was that?" For the old guys, the second round was just confirmation to run as fast as we could to the nearest bunker. What was Charlie doing—didn't he hear that I had an early drop and was going home? After the "all clear" was given, everyone moved out of the bunker to survey the damage. Well, almost everyone. I was not moving until I was completely confident that the "all clear" was for real.

Four or five 122mm rockets had slammed into our area. The damage was greater to the battalion area than our company area. We resumed our normal day's routine, but word filtered down that the spring offensive had begun, and we could expect a ground and rocket attack that Wednesday night. From my previous experience of catching the enemy with a map of Minuteman Manor, I figured they had a detailed plan. I weighed my options, one of which was to sleep in one of the bunkers and hope the VC sappers didn't lob a few grenades into that bunker after we scrambled for them. I decided against that and instead chose to take a mattress and my M1 carbine and camp out on the roof of my hooch. I was not going to wait in a bunker to die. I would pull sentry duty to protect myself and stay up all night if need be. I had two packs of unfiltered Lucky Strikes, a couple of candy bars, and enough ammo to hold off whatever came at me. All night I stayed awake, just watching and waiting. At one point, an actual sentry patrol walked by my hooch and I almost shot him.

Dawn finally arrived and I had survived the potential attack, or so I thought. I climbed down from my rooftop perch and crawled into my bunk, thinking I could get a few hours of sleep before I made the final arrangements to get out of there. My head hit the pillow, and I was out like a light. It couldn't have been more than fifteen minutes before I heard the whine of the incoming rocket. I was in the bunker before any of my fellow pilots came diving in. Among others, I was joined by Captain Boen, who was also leaving that day. We looked at each other in disbelief—*how could this be happening to us?*

Finally, the time had come to take the C-130 to Cam Ranh Bay and then a flight back to the real world. We out-processed at Cam Ranh and were told that the flight out was the next morning at 0900. We had lots of time to kill, and the hours seemed to drag on. Luckily at night, sleep made the time go by faster. In all the time Cam Ranh Bay had been in existence, they had had maybe three or four rocket or mortar attacks. I was lucky enough to be part of the fifth.

Captain Boen was hot on my tail as we made it to a culvert, which was their idea of a bunker. We looked at each other again in disbelief, only this time he said, "You really are a magnet-ass, aren't you?"

I replied, "Yes, but a lucky magnet-ass. Stay with me and some of it will rub off on you." He took that to heart wherever I went.

As the Flying Tiger 707 reached takeoff speed and wheels up, all of us on the plane let out a collective yell and cheer. We were going home.

I ARRIVED AT Fort Lewis, Washington, for out-processing. The date was May 2. Two days later on May 4, 1970, members of the Ohio National Guard fired into a crowd of Kent State University demonstrators, killing four students and wounding nine others. They had been protesting the war I had just survived. Sadly, they were not as lucky.

WAYNE CHASSON

PART 4:

HOME AND BEYOND

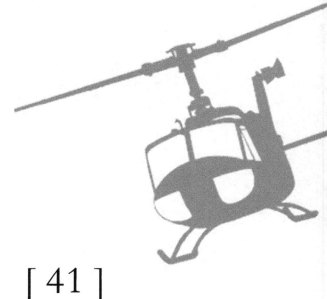

[41]

SO CLOSE, BUT NOW

WHAT?

MY FEET WERE firmly on U.S. soil. I was only two days away from freedom because I was two days from being out of the Army. My first order of business was to call my mom and dad. They could relax now, I was really home.

Rather than lugging home the clothes I had bought in Hong Kong, I mailed them before I left Vietnam. I also sent a letter to my parents asking them to unpack the boxes when they arrived to prevent my new clothes from developing permanent wrinkles. I called them as soon as I landed in Seattle. Our conversation covered the usual: I was home, I was almost a free man, what did I want for my first meal, and so on. I was talking to both of them at the same time, one on one extension and one on another. My mother started her side of the conversation.

"You know the boxes you wanted us to open?" she asked.

"Yes."

"Well, we only opened one."

"What? Why not all of them?" I asked.

"Well, your father and I started with the first box, and I came to this green folder, opened it and said, 'Is this what I think it is?'" The green folder was an award for a Purple Heart. "We dug a little deeper and came to another green folder, and it was a second Purple Heart. So we stopped right there and left the rest of the box untouched."

"Well," I said, "it's a good thing you didn't go any further because there was one more." There was dead silence from both of them. I quickly filled the emptiness, "But I'm home now and I will explain everything when I get back." We ended the conversation with kisses and the promise that I would call them the minute I knew my travel arrangements—no more surprises. To this day I still believe I had made the right decision early on. I never wanted my parents to constantly worry about my safety. They would be reminded every week in the news as to how many young Americans had died that week. If they thought I was a maintenance pilot then I wouldn't be in harm's way and maybe just maybe that would ease their fears.

During out-processing from the Army, we had to go through a certain amount of paperwork, and they still wanted us to represent the image of a good soldier. The sergeant major handling my out-processing said, "Sir, the colonel will never approve that haircut, it's too long."

I said, "But I'm getting out of the Army forever. Can't I go home looking like a civilian?"

"Sorry, sir. He won't do it," he said.

Begrudgingly, I walked off to find the post barber. This was the last thing I wanted. I had a great tan, fashionably medium length hair, and it was the beginning of May. But once in the barbershop, I did as told and asked for a haircut that the colonel would approve of in order for him to sign my release papers. I sat in the chair watching my civilian haircut fade back into an Army haircut. I was pissed. I hustled back to the sergeant major's desk and asked, "Okay, does this pass for a haircut? And when can I see the colonel to sign the papers?"

"Oh, that won't be necessary sir. I can sign the papers – the colonel is out of the office," he said.

Now I was really pissed. He did that on purpose. Just like all the other sergeant majors in the Army, their job is "haircuts and uniforms." You know how the difference between a good haircut and a bad haircut is two weeks? This haircut needed *four* weeks before it could be considered a good haircut. I walked out of the sergeant major's office, hoping he would rot in hell.

I had tickets in hand and called my parents with the airline and arrival times. I had one stop in Chicago, then on to Boston. I sat in the Seattle-Tacoma airport waiting for my flight, just like I had seven months earlier on Christmas Eve.

With all I had been through the last eighteen months, a little more hardship wouldn't kill me. Once on the plane I ended up in a middle seat. To my right was a young man whose hair was down to his shoulders. I thought of what the sergeant major could do with that head of hair. To my left was the largest man I had ever seen, squeezed into the seat and requiring two seat belts. He was so big that when he went to plug in his headphones for the two music stations they offered, he didn't have enough room for his and ended up using mine.

There I was, trapped in the middle like a sardine—but I was going *home*, and I would keep my eye on the prize. The flight attendant came over to me as I was dozing to ask if I wanted anything. I startled, not expecting this, and nearly came out of my seat thinking she was a Viet Cong who had followed me to the States. I must have scared the living shit out of her because she jumped back with a look that said, *Oh God, please don't kill me.* I apologized but offered no explanation. Later I dozed off again, and she had to come back to tell me to fasten my seatbelt. Same scenario—I nearly came out of my skin and she almost did as well. Again, I apologized with no explanation, though by now I was a bit embarrassed.

From Chicago, we headed to Boston with the same flight crew.

This time, she was prepared. When she had to wake me again, she approached from the row behind me. As we deplaned and I walked out, she looked even more relieved than I was to be in Boston.

From Boston it was on to Cape Cod, which was to be my new home for the next four months or so.

MY DAD HAD talked to a friend who ran a local bar called Your Father's Moustache. It was a perfect summer job. The people I worked with occasionally would ask how I had such a great tan so early in the summer. I was a bit of a newbie, but after a while I didn't stick out that much. I can thank Cathy Serrato and the other great people I worked with for the easy transition.

My parents' house was on a salt-water pond in Dennis, Massachusetts. It had a little cabin set off in the woods where I could spend my nights. If I happened to have company with me, the walk of shame was in front of the family room of the main house, which was all glass. Nevertheless, my parents made whatever adjustments they could to make me feel guilt-free.

I remember sitting in the family room of my parents' house with my sister Ellen one day, casually talking, when I heard a gunshot from just off the lake. I hit the floor thinking the VC had followed me home. "How did they know where I lived?" I thought. My sister jumped up from her chair and immediately went outside to yell at the idiot that just scared the shit out of her little brother.

What were they thinking shooting off a rifle in a residential neighborhood? They must have thought she was crazy, but they apologized and said that it wouldn't happen again. When she came back in I said, "Once a magnet-ass, always a magnet-ass." There was no explanation on my part of what a magnet- ass was, just a look from her that said, *It's all right now.*

FAST EDDY COVILL showed up at the house about three weeks after my return home. It was great to see him. We spent a week talking, fishing, and sailing the salt-water pond. As we said our goodbyes, we promised we would try to stay in touch, but that never happened.

I've mentioned the bond of brothers at war—It was us and our fellow crewmembers against the world. All we wanted to do was survive. When the war ended, it was something we put behind us. There were no connections with past crew members, just each of us holding on to our shared memories. I can recall stories and picture the faces of Dave Young, Ed Covill, Steve Kerchenfaunt, and many others just as they were during those two short and intense years between 1968 and 1970. It's strange that we were such a tight group of guys then, yet after the war we seldom had contact. Part of me didn't want to relive the bad memories, the terror, the loss of friends. Putting it behind me was a way of dealing with the flashbacks and nightmares—I might have thought rekindling the brotherhood would just prolong the pain.

JUST AS I was settling in at home, in May of 1970, President Nixon decided to invade part of Cambodia. That area was a major supply route for the NVA into the southern area of Vietnam. During that time, my parents had a fairly large group of relatives visiting who presumed that I would have a better understanding of why we were going into Cambodia. I didn't have any insight to give them. I had already had my own little war, and as far as I was concerned that was the only thing I had been involved with. I think they sensed my uneasiness, and perhaps got a look from my mother, so that was the end of the conversation.

I had no answer about war then, and I don't have one now. Was it the misguided decision-making of generals and politicians? Body count seemed the main objective, not the taking and holding of territory—Having to take Hamburger Hill several times only to leave it after a few days never made any sense. Was it due to the lack of support back home? Maybe if the population of the United States was asked to make the same sacrifices they did during World Wars I and II, things might have been different. I'm sure the real answer is complicated, but my part wasn't complicated. It was one day at a time in my own little cocoon.

I didn't have any one I could talk to about the Vietnam War. I felt it was a mess. No good outcome was going to justify 58,000 lives lost and many, many, more wounded in spirit and body. Even if someone was open to a discussion about the war, how could I explain it to them if they hadn't been there? I certainty couldn't argue *for* the war but I didn't want someone telling me what was right if they hadn't walked in a soldiers shoes.

A FINAL NOTE on the Vietnam War: For the most part, the last American combat troops pulled out in August 1972. The North Vietnamese rolled into Saigon in April of 1975. News coverage showed helicopters airlifting hundreds of desperate people on April 29, and video footage showed helicopters being pushed off Navy ships, off the coast of Vietnam, to make room for hundreds of refugees trying to escape the incoming North Vietnamese Army. What had we accomplished?

They say that war is about soldiers who love their country. I feel that, more importantly, it is about soldiers who love one another. Moments of hell don't leave you neutral. You can't be untouched by it—you see it, live it, experience it, and it will be with you forever. For me, the end of the war brought no emotion—it was simply a part of my life that was over. I just tried to hide my lack of emotion as best I could. In reality, the war had ended for me in May of 1970 when I left and all I wanted was to put the war behind me.

Just as I returned stateside on May 4, 1970, members of the Ohio National Guard fired into a crowd of Kent State University demonstrators, killing four and wounding nine Kent State students. My reaction was, *What could have triggered this event?* Did a guardsmen feel threatened by the protesters? Was there a backfire from a car that prompted the volley of fire? Did the protesters cross the line from peaceful to antagonist? Were there those in the crowd that wanted to incite a riot, not measuring the consequences? For me I couldn't make a judgment as to right or wrong. I wasn't walking in anybody's shoes. I didn't scorn either side, I didn't resent either side, I just couldn't justify the loss of life. The soldiers might have just been doing what they had been told to do. The protesters thought they could help bring an end to the war. Depending on one's point of view, no right, no wrong. The impact of these shootings was dramatic, triggering a nationwide student strike that forced hundreds of colleges and universities to close for a short time, and that hastened the end of the war in Vietnam.

EAGER TO GET on with my life I enrolled at Wentworth Institute of Technology. They offered a program in aviation science technology. I thought I could continue my love of flying with their help. It was quite an adjustment being five months removed from flying in Vietnam to a classroom full of eighteen-year-old students. They were all about college life and I was adjusting to hours and hours of studying. I thought I would never be able to handle the academics. After the first semester I found my grades to be honor roll worthy, a surprise based on my previous college years. Amazing what focus and hard work can do for you.

After my first year, Northeastern had a new program for those who wanted to fly and combine that skill with a Bachelor of Science degree. I took the leap and transferred, which started yet another chapter in my life with my love of flying, because the program also trained you as a fixed-wing airplane pilot. And I did have a funny incident early on in my flight training. I was training on small Cessna aircraft out of Norwood, Massachusetts. This one particular day getting ready for takeoff with my instructor, I was taxiing down the ramp for the takeoff when I noticed a Volkswagen Beetle heading in my direction. He was paying more attention to a biplane that had landed an hour earlier. It was unusual to have a regular traffic vehicle driving on this part of the ramp, even if they worked at the airfield.

As he got closer I taxied farther to the right to avoid his car. I moved as much as I could to the right but was limited by other aircraft parked on that side. The driver was apparently still focused on the biplane and not on me. I was as close to the parked aircraft as I could be without causing damage to them when I finally said to my instructor, "I don't think he sees us."

With that my instructor diverted his attention from whatever he was doing and said, "Holy Shit."

The wing of my small Cessna collided with the top of the beetle and sheared off the top, turning his Volkswagen sedan into a convertible. I had several thoughts in that instant—one, did we hit the wings' gas tanks? If so let's get the hell out of this airplane. And two, was the driver alive, as I could no longer see him? And additionally, did I make it all the way back from Vietnam only to die in a plane on the ground?

Pushing the startled instructor out of the way I raced over to the vehicle to find the hapless driver slumped to the passenger's seat. He had seen my aircraft a milli-second before impact and ducked down just in time. He was going to be alright, just a few cuts and bruises and major embarrassment. I reached inside his new convertible to shut off his car radio that was blaring a song by Chicago. I didn't want him to lose his battery as well as his pride. I wondered later on how he was going to explain to his insurance company that he got in an accident with a plane.

The rest of my flight training was uneventful. I finished off my Bachelor of Science degree with Northeastern University. Fortunately or unfortunately, working my way through school with the VA's help, I started to know more about the working of the restaurant business and flying took a back seat.

[42]

THE MASSACHUSETTS

ARMY NATIONAL GUARD

FAST-FORWARD TO 1976, I was living on the Cape and happened to be walking through the mall one day when I saw a display for the Massachusetts Army National Guard. I wondered for a minute if this could be for me. There were brochures for joining, one of which promoted flying in the Guard. I talked to a few of the Guard ambassadors, and the most important question I had was whether I could get out of the Guard if I wanted to.

"Oh sure," they told me, "you can quit whenever you want."

That scared me, because I didn't believe it for a second. Jimmy Carter had just been elected the 39th president and his inexperience had me concerned for the future of the country. I thought better of it and put thought of the National Guard aside for the time being.

Four years later, having moved to Boston I was working at the Seaside Restaurant and Bar in Quincy Market. One night, two patrons happened to start talking about flying. I asked if they were pilots, and the conversation was off and running. Dave Mason and Sandy Reed were, in fact, helicopter pilots and were in the Massachusetts National Guard. They loved being in the Guard. They said it was like a flying club, and I should look into it. Jimmy Carter was no longer the president, and I had no idea what was in store for us with Ronald Reagan, but I decided to take the plunge, so to speak.

I had recently married my first wife Maureen while working at the Seaside restaurant. We made our way as newlyweds through the early years of marriage, living and working in Boston. My brother asked if I would consider going into the restaurant business with him on Cape Cod. Maureen and I had planned on starting a family and thought the Cape offered a better environment for raising children. I joined the National Guard in December 1980, though I didn't officially make it to my first drill until February of 1981—the first of many drill weekends to come.

I was relieved to learn that I was not the only former pilot who wondered if he could still fly. That first weekend I met another newbie, Dwight Howard from Hanson, Massachusetts. At first I thought he was a grizzled veteran because of his shocking white hair. In fact, he was actually a tad younger than I but he too loved and missed flying. He was a former Vietnam pilot who had gotten out of the Army in 1972, and we were both feeling out this new career choice, still unsure if it was the right decision.

The Aviation Brigade at Otis AFB on the Cape was made up of UH-I Hueys and the OH-6 Loach, today's "little bird." Based on my prior experience, I was given the opportunity to fly the Huey. As much as I loved the Huey, the opportunity to fly something different was exciting, and the Loach intrigued me. The Loach platoon had eight aircraft, and the flying profile was basically, "You're on your own." The small "little bird" was an amazingly responsive helicopter to flight inputs. You could practically just think about a left or right turn and the helicopter would do it.

Years later I remember describing the different aircraft I had flown to someone. The Huey was the trusted family station wagon of the fifties and sixties. The Black Hawk was about as agile as a giant bus. The Little Bird was a stripped-down version of the MGB sports car you always wanted to drive. With the doors off, it was like the MGB with the top down.

One month later Geoff Boehm, another Vietnam vet, joined the same unit, and the three of us became fast friends. Geoff had been with First Cavalry in Nam and was proud to show everyone his giant Cav patch on his right shoulder. A patch on your left shoulder signified what unit you were presently with. The right shoulder patch was reserved for the combat unit you had been with. When he would walk up to a group of new guardsmen he kind of flicked his right shoulder towards the group as to say, "Hi, I'm Geoff and I was part of the First Cav." As a member of the Cav Geoff could get away with it. The American division, of which Dwight and I had been a part, didn't hold the same mystique. He was also quick to show pictures of his standard Cav mustache, a symbol of pride with the First Cav.

In the Guard we supported a unit called Division Artillery, but I don't think they knew what to do with us. The Guard had the assets, but no plan for best utilizing the helicopter. That was fine for Dwight, Geoff, and me, because once we had qualified in the aircraft, we were free to make things up as we went along. Everything came rushing back to me. It was exhilarating, to say the least. An additional benefit to the experience was that they were paying me to fly. I didn't tell them this, of course, but I almost would have paid them if it had come down to it.

I had the great pleasure of being with many weekend warriors who enjoyed the camaraderie as much as I did. It was a grind at times, with weekends away from the family, but the Guard became my weekend family. And since my house was only twenty-five minutes from the base, I tried to fly every opportunity I had.

Dwight and I spent a great deal of time flying together. During one conversation I discovered that when he was in Vietnam he had been assigned to the 176th AHC. *What a small world.* We had missed each other by a mere nine months. We continued to build our skills together, and at one point the facility commander chose us to represent the Massachusetts Army National Guard at the World Helicopter Championship. We practiced every chance we could. Unfortunately, the funds for our travel and expenses fell under the axe of the budget for the state and that was the end of that. We created our own niche for training and came up with some clever training scenarios. We loved the Loach, as well as the fact that people still didn't know what to do with us and left us alone.

The Guard played a vital role in my life. Being in the Guard, nobody shot at me, which was a definite plus, but there were some interesting moments, nevertheless. The Aviation Brigade was so large that the drill weekends were often split between the Hueys and Loaches on one weekend and the battalion maintenance company on another. Once a quarter, however, all personnel would show up for the same drill weekend. On one of these drill weekends, I noticed a pilot from the maintenance company who looked familiar, but I couldn't quite place him or recall his name. He had a big afro, which looked out of place in the Guard since none of the other pilots had hair quite that bushy. Probably six months later, I noticed the combat patch on his right shoulder. I finally said to him, "Hey, when you were in Vietnam, what company were you with?"

He said, matter-of-factly, "The 176th AHC."

I said, "I was your copilot on the day you were wounded at Tien Fuck." It was Barry Lamkin. He looked at me in total amazement. I filled him in on what had happened that day after I took the controls, though I left out the part about my feet remaining firmly planted to the helicopter floor. I don't think I ever ran into him again on drill weekends. He eventually left the Guard. I guess that part about getting out whenever you wanted wasn't so unbelievable after all.

FLYING WITH DWIGHT we were always in control, by which I mean we never did any "hot dog" stuff. If I wanted to do something on the edge, Dwight would always be there to say, "You know, you might want to think twice about this." I would reconsider, but at the same time he trusted my judgment completely. There were some great pilots in the Guard. Wendy Moore probably could have flown a bathtub if it had rotor blades, and Kenny Clive could make the Loach do just about anything he wanted. They were in a league of their own.

Dwight was one of the best pilots I have ever flown with. Aviation-wise, we thought alike, and when we would do single pilot formation flights through New York City, it was as though we were in the same aircraft talking things out. Flying through New York City with one UHF radio trying to talk to approach control was about as challenging as it got. We made a great team.

The whole Loach platoon with Geoff and Dwight as my sidekicks was great. We flew with some outstanding crew chiefs. The camaraderie from Vietnam was evident in just about everything we did—even though none of the crew chiefs had been in Vietnam. It was the way we looked out for them, and they looked out for us. We always had each other's backs. We taught all the crew chiefs to fly when the opportunity presented itself. One crew chief, Dan Pacheco, could fly the Loach as though he had been born in it.

On some of the annual training periods, Dwight, Geoff, and I would be out flying Loaches and would use names from a current television show so as not to let anyone know who we were. Just like the characters from the Bob Newhart show who introduce themselves: "Hi, I'm Larry, and this is my brother Darryl, and this is my other brother Darryl," I would call to Larry in the "blind," and Dwight or Geoff were sure to answer. We knew whose attention we were trying to get, but the units on the ground had no clue.

WHILE I HAD been away from aviation, the Army adopted some new flying tactics. One such tactic was known as NOE or "nap of the earth" flying. We would fly around at the speed of a walk, masking or hiding ourselves from the enemy. The idea was that the threat environment we would be flying into was much different than it had been in Vietnam. The danger was not so much AK-47s but bigger caliber weapons, some of them radar-controlled. Specifically, this was the threat the Russians posed. I had trouble adjusting to this theory. I understood the threat of the heavy weapons, but I also thought that flying around at that speed and altitude over the enemy would get us killed just as easily with a small bullet as a big bullet.

On one occasion during drill weekend, I was flying a smoke ship mission with Pete Minnar. He wasn't a former Vietnam pilot, but he was a really likeable guy who made flying fun. We were flying the smoke ship, which was a Loach helicopter set up with an oil tank in the back of the aircraft. A tube from the oil tank was directed onto the hot exhaust from the engine, and a thick white cloud of smoke would pour out. In Vietnam, the intent of a smoke mission was for a helicopter to come down on a CA, flying five or ten feet off the terrain, and lay down the smoke – that way, the enemy might not see the slicks making their approach or landing. We flew about as fast as we could so that we wouldn't get shot down.

On this particular day, Pete was hovering around, laying down the smoke at the speed of a walk, not aware of gunfire tactics. I finally said, "I'm not sure what we're trying to accomplish."

He said, "What do you mean?"

I said, "If this were real life, we would be dead by now."

He asked me to show him how we used to do it. I zigged and zagged over the ground unit's position at a fairly high rate of speed.

Once finished, I said, "That's what will keep you alive, not flying over the enemy at ten feet, at a speed that begs for a shoot down." I think I convinced him that the Army's take on the new ways of tactical flying were suicide.

For a few years, Otis AFB would entertain the public with either the Navy Blue Angels or the Air Force Thunderbirds. This was an exciting time that became even more so for me because I would fly a Loach demonstration. As the date of the event drew near, I would practice a series of maneuvers that I hoped the crowd would remember. I knew they all came to see the Angels or Thunderbirds, but I hoped I could entertain them as well, at least in a small way.

One year, I raced down the airfield at the very top speed a Loach could do, as low as I could get without making my state aviation officer nervous. The area along the runway had a very shallow ditch running parallel to it and was on the far side of the crowd. I positioned the helicopter in the depression and flew as fast as I could. To the crowd, it looked like I was just a few inches from hitting the ground, when actually I had three or four feet. At the end of my run, I would pull back on the cyclic, pull pitch at the same time, and climb as though I had been shot out of a cannon. Once at altitude, I dove back down and stopped a few feet from the ground. It made for a few "oohs" and "ahs." I also had the smoke machine on board. I positioned myself in front of the crowd, and the air show announcer said, "Watch this, folks." Then I started a spinning climb and hit the smoke generator. The only problem was, the cockpit filled with smoke as I was climbing, which made for a momentary "oh shit" moment. As I got to the top of my demonstration turns, I had to brace my leg up against the collective to allow a free hand to turn off the smoke!

Before my demonstration during another airshow, I had been down at the other end of the airfield and out of sight from the crowd practicing the cyclic climbs. At that end of the airfield, the direction of the climbs and the wind were, unbeknownst to me, different from what I would be using during the actual demonstration run. During my act, therefore, when I got to the top of the climb, there was a momentary hesitation on the part of the Loach. It didn't want to turn in the direction I had planned or practiced. The helicopter wanted to go left, and I wanted to go right. I started to stall, and I had visions of crashing the helicopter in front of thousands of people. I recovered, but after I landed, Dwight, who had been watching, came up to me and said, "You cut that a little close, didn't you?"

I told him about the wind direction change and asked, "Do you think it looked good, and do you think the state aviation officer noticed?"

"Yes, and let's hope not," was his reply. I had to tame down any air shows I did after that.

IT WAS ABOUT this time that the National Guard decided the Loach was no longer going to be part of its inventory, and we had to turn in all the Loaches we had. On two or three occasions, I was assigned to transfer a Loach down to Navy Lakehurst, New Jersey. It's quite a challenge flying through New York City with only a UHF radio. Normally most aircraft would have several radios for communication with airports, control zones, or other aircraft. We had just two, and airports and control zones usually talked on a VHF radio, an altogether different frequency. You couldn't enter certain airspaces without first establishing radio communication. The challenge of finding a radio frequency that ground operators would monitor in busy New York airspace was frustrating to say the least.

After landing, we were met by three men wearing dark navy blazers and packing 9mm pistols under their jackets. We were then escorted to a small room where we were told to wait. After a couple of hours, we were told we were clear to leave. The trail aircraft that had followed us down was our ride home. All this secrecy led us to believe that the CIA was apparently getting some of our Loaches. I'm sure they put those "little birds" to great use.

On one occasion I was assigned to transport a Loach, single-pilot, to Oklahoma. Dick Mongeau, a great facility maintenance person, was assigned to join me and take care of maintenance issues. Dick had been around for quite a while but his expertise was maintenance and not the nuances of flying a cross-country flight. Thinking back, other than a pilot, I can think of no better a person to be with. I spent days planning the cross-country flight, with navigation to, or near, military facilities, which allowed for fuel and any potential maintenance issues that might come up. Dick and I started out in late October 1985. We made a great team. The cockpit was full of maps and snacks. The first quarter of the route I was familiar with, having done cross-country trips through New York and Pennsylvania before.

We spent the first night in West Virginia. We got up the next morning, ready to beat a weather system that was moving in. It was the remnants of Hurricane Juan, which had come ashore in Louisiana, looped around back to the Gulf, and was then working its way up the southeastern U.S. We had the weather to go but ran into a problem starting the aircraft. It seemed this bird would only start with a ground power assist, which I had been unaware of. This delay set us back three hours. I checked weather again before takeoff and was assured that we would be okay.

Normally, we would want to be at least a few thousand feet high for navigation landmarks. The weather was not as reported to me earlier. I was led to believe the flight conditions would be suitable for visual flight rules which meant I could fly at altitude to find my way on this leg of the flight by landmarks. That was not the case. The cloud cover was such that we had to keep getting lower in altitude, and visibility was declining rapidly. I was flying with a navigational sectional map on my lap, and Dick had a road atlas in his. We were low enough to read the highway signs. As pilots, we jokingly said IFR was also known as, "I Follow Roads." Well, we put that to the test. We even made use of signs that said, "Next city, x number of miles."

I must say, central Kentucky, with its horse farms and miles of white fencing, is, if possible, even more beautiful from the air. But as we came into Louisville, the weather was below minimums for any aircraft flying into the Louisville Bowman airport. We couldn't just stop in mid-air waiting for clearance to get into the airport. We were low on fuel, so I deemed this an emergency. I decided to land in a field void of any horses and wait for our special clearance into the airport control zone. Finally, with clearance from the tower, we were allowed to proceed and land at Louisville Bowman airport.

Two days later, it appeared we had sufficient visibility and cloud ceiling to continue our journey. We checked with the weather specialists, and they assured us the weather would be above the minimums needed to make our next leg. Once again, they weren't quite accurate with their report. We were somewhere in Arkansas, following a highway at low level, when we hit a torrential downpour. I had tractor-trailers driving down the highway passing by me, as though my little Loach were standing still. I was practically hovering, trying to find an airport where we could land. After a while I said to Dick, "This is crazy. I'm going to put the helicopter down."

He reminded me we only had about thirty minutes on the ground in order to restart the aircraft, or we would be stuck. I decided to gamble on shutting the helicopter down, hoping that it wouldn't be more than thirty minutes. I spotted a farmhouse and put the bird down as cows and horses ran in all directions. Wondering what in the world I was doing, a farmer, probably in his seventies, came out and asked what was wrong and what he could do to help. I asked, "Do you have a phone, and do you have friends in the area who might give me an eyewitness account of the weather ahead?"

We were on a plateau, and I thought if I could get to the valley below we might make it under the weather. He said, "Sure, come on inside."

Dick and I met his wife, and I was directed to the phone on a small table across from the family couch. Dick sat down between the farmer and his wife while I made the call. The farmer's mother lived about four miles or so down the road in the direction we wanted to go. I explained our situation with regard to the weather and our destination. She was eager to help. I asked her if she was familiar with and if she could see any of her neighbors' houses. I was trying to determine the visibility. She said something like, "I can see Billy Bob's house."

I said, "Good, how far away is his house?"

She replied, "Across the street."

Not enough, I thought. "How about some other landmark or house that is a little further away?"

She came back with, "Well, there is the church about a quarter of a mile away."

"Great," I said, "how clearly can you see that?"

"Oh, I can't see that at all."

I thanked her and told her she had been a big help. I hung up the phone and thought, *This is not going to work*, and with that, put my head in my hands. The farmer looked at me and said without hesitation, "I think that's a good idea, son. We'll all pray." He grabbed Dick's one hand, while his wife took Dick's other hand and started to pray. I was looking out of the corner of my eye at Dick, thinking, *Well, I've tried everything else, let's give this a shot.*

We walked back to the helicopter within the thirty minutes, and I kept my fingers crossed. It started, much to my relief, and now I only had to hope that God would make a small clearing in the sky so we could go on. He did, and we made Mountain View, Missouri. I said to Dick, "That's as far as we are going to push our luck."

Some of the townsfolk came out to catch a rare glimpse of a helicopter and offer whatever assistance they could. They couldn't have been more gracious and helpful. We ate at a local bowling alley, with all the residents asking what they could do to help. We needed lodging, so that was our next stop. It was Halloween night, and we spent the evening in a little six-unit hotel. It was going to be heaven to both of us. Of course, we did get some trick-or-treaters, but without any candy, I started passing out one-dollar bills. I think they were a little disappointed with the money.

The next morning, we still faced the task of getting the Loach started. Dick enlisted two pickup trucks, parked them side-by-side, and on the word "go," I pulled the trigger for starting while he started running in a circle with a rotor blade in hand, trying to take the load off the engine. It worked. We waved goodbye, took off, and circled back with a low flyby, wagging our tail boom, and headed for Cape Girardeau, Missouri, hoping for better weather ahead.

We did get a little better weather, but only enough to allow us to get to 500 feet altitude. Dick and I went over the planned route of flight for the day, and this one had us IFR—this time meaning, "I Follow Railroads." But there was a hitch to this plan. The railroad we were following suddenly disappeared. I had to make a quick decision to either go back and pick up the railroad again to see where we got off course, or to return to Cape Girardeau and refuel, starting all over again. I decided the railroad couldn't just vanish, so we doubled back. Sure enough, the railroad was gone, but the railroad bed that the tracks had been on was still there, so we followed that. It was the right decision and just as we approached Springfield, Missouri, the sky opened up and it was "clear blue and 22" (an expression for great aviation weather).

After the run to Tulsa, Oklahoma, it was back to the Cape. All the Loaches had been turned in, and I was back in a Huey. It was like finding that old pair of blue jeans that fit so well, and when I strapped in after all those years the lived-in comfort level just felt so right. Dwight and I worked on high overhead approaches because it had been so long since I last did one. In the four-bladed Loach, we couldn't do them because the blades would pick up too much speed in the descent. The two-bladed Huey had no such issues, and the approaches all came rushing back.

I was a PIC (pilot in command) in the Huey, so I had the opportunity to fly with pilots who no longer needed an instructor pilot. I felt that they should know what Geoff, Dwight, and I knew about tactics. The three big maneuvers were the quick stop, contour flying, and of course the high overhead. The contour came easy once we explained what to look for, and just as importantly how it should feel in your butt as you were flying—It had a feeling almost like slalom skiing, and if we were being thrown from side-to-side in our seat, it wasn't right. Mike Madigan and Matt Cummings took to it best. The high overhead took more time. The maneuver seemed almost out of control at first, and even though there wasn't much opportunity to practice this maneuver, they gradually picked up the idea of what we were trying to accomplish, and it started to come together.

SOME TWELVE OR FIFTEEN years later, I had two surprise visitors. I owned a restaurant in Hyannis, Massachusetts, at the time, and a fellow walked in who wanted to see the owner about a job. I came out to tell the prospective employee that we had a full staff, and I was sorry I couldn't help him out. He said to me, "But I can make really good cakes, in a frying pan, no less."

10—Our BoSox company patch

I was stopped in my tracks. Nobody makes cakes in a frying pan, I thought, unless they learned to do it in Vietnam. I looked closely, almost not recognizing that it was Steve Kerchenfaunt, who was traveling the country and wanted to see me. As tall as ever with a few more pounds put on, you take the boy out of Ohio but you couldn't take Ohio out of Steve. He still had that innocent smile and almost a bashfulness to his voice.

I couldn't believe that this former crewmember, one who I had felt was an extension of me, was standing in my restaurant pretending to ask for a job. We talked for a while, trying to catch up, but how do you catch up in an hour on what happened then and what has happened since? We said our goodbyes, promising to stay in touch. Steve sent a Christmas card every year for a while, but I simply tried to put that life behind me. It wasn't just forgetting that time in my life, I had a wife and family not to mention the struggles of running a restaurant. There was no time to relive the past. I regret the poor correspondent that I was. It remains one of my biggest sources of shame.

Sometime later, Fast Eddy showed up at the restaurant. I had joined the National Guard in Massachusetts, and Ed had joined the Guard in Connecticut. He happened to be spending his two-week annual training period at Otis AFB on the Cape and asked around as to where I might be. One of my fellow guardsmen told him I was at a restaurant in Hyannis. As usual, Fast Eddy held court at the bar in the restaurant, telling stories that embarrassed me yet entertained everyone else. He filled me in on what he was up to in the civilian world and when we said our goodbyes, we both knew it would only be by chance that we would ever meet up again.

THERE IS AN organization called the Vietnam Helicopters Pilot Association that has a reunion every year. I know some who have gone from time to time, but I never have. I have always been somewhat shy or at least quiet, never a particularly good storyteller, and I honestly didn't think I would recognize any of their aging faces.

One summer, the moving wall of the Vietnam Memorial came to Hyannis. It's a replica of the monument in D.C. and it was here for four or five days and then traveled on to other parts of the country. I knew it had been well-received throughout its travels, but initially I just couldn't bring myself to see it firsthand. Finally, one night after the restaurant closed and I knew the streets of Hyannis would be deserted, I walked down to where it was on display. It was probably two in the morning. I was the only one there. Even in its small scale, it was a sobering tribute and experience.

I sat there in silence at first just looking at its small-scale eloquence.

Making a powerful statement without being able to speak. I slowly approached the wall looking to find the soldiers I had served with, hoping to touch their names. We never had the chance to say goodbye to the dead, they were just taken from us. Now it was my turn. Maybe it was survivor's remorse—I was alive, they forever would be immortalized on a piece of granite. Even though it was summer, there seemed to be a chill to the night air. I slowly turned to leave my "buddies," knowing I would never forget what I had and what they sacrificed.

My sister-in-law lives in Falls Church, Virginia. I had been there several times but never had the courage to make the trip to the Washington D.C. Vietnam Memorial. After having seen the moving wall in Hyannis, I knew that it was my duty to finally visit the real wall. It was my obligation and privilege to pay my respects to Dee Hyden and all my other fallen comrades of the 176th AHC* along with all others who died during the war. Everything about the wall is dignified and respectful. For those who served and for all that we went through during that time, the wall is a final salute to those who gave their lives. It's not about the "right and wrong" of the war, but simply a chance to remember and say goodbye. Some 2.5 million served in Vietnam, and some 58,000 of those died. The war that was supposed to be over in eight weeks exceeded that timetable in sacrifices never imagined.

*Dee Hyden

Don Stockton

Larry Keeler

Don Rose

William Barritt

Bruce Shaffer

Angus McAllister

Merle Butler

Rich Ford

WAYNE CHASSON

John Bailey

Ralph Bigelow

Mike Pickles

[43]

AGR

BECAUSE I ENJOYED what I was doing in the Guard, and to take the pressure off the ups and downs of owning a seasonal restaurant on Cape Cod, I had been actively seeking a full-time National Guard job. Unfortunately, the budget didn't hold much promise for my future Guard plans. However, while volunteering at my children's school I got the bug to teach. At the insistence of one my children's teacher's I went back to get another degree in education. I wound up teaching fifth grade at a Barnstable school and loved it. There was no single subject to focus on. It was a challenge, schooling ten and eleven-year-old children in math, English, science and whatever the curriculum demanded.

My fellow teachers were great, and principal Tom Macdonald was an inspiration—someone I definitely wanted to excel for. I had only been teaching two years when the Army Guard Reserve of the Massachusetts Army National Guard had an opening for a training officer. I had thoroughly enjoyed teaching and loved the age of the fifth-graders, but a teacher's salary was a third of what I could make with the Guard full-time. I had my family to think of.

My now second wife Mary and I had five children who were either in college or soon to be bound for a higher institute for learning. Financially this would be a daunting task at best, impossible if we hoped to cover all their expenses. I applied and was accepted into a full-time position. Prior to securing the training officer position, in addition to the seasonal restaurant in Hyannis, my wife and I had recently purchased The Barnacle snack bar on Craigville Beach on Cape Cod, also seasonal. I had worked in the restaurant business ever since I returned from Vietnam. For a person in their early twenties it was carefree and easy meeting lots of people. In the later stages of my life, owning a restaurant was a challenge that would task my body and soul—long hours, never sure if you could meet payroll that week, a struggle to survive. Grinding my teeth as I slept only added to those trying years. I would add another layer onto my already busy life but one that would insure a guaranteed income. It was not uncommon in the season to work one hundred hours a week. Yet in all these hours, I worked with great staff that made life pleasurable if not stress-free.

Being selected for the training officer position was like hitting the lottery. The pay was very good, and I got paid every two weeks and on time. In the restaurant business I was the last to get paid, and that was only if there was money left after expenses to pay myself at all.

I was bound and determined not to let down any of the people who had faith in me. Coming from the restaurant world, where working sixty and seventy hours a week was not uncommon, I was ready to work any number of hours. As I mentioned before Judy Halstead was my readiness NCO and a great teacher and mentor. At first there was so much to learn. It was far different from anything I had previously done in the Guard, especially more administrative work. But with Judy's help I slowly started to get the hang of things.

I worked with some great people at the base: Judy, Steve Bethoney, Bob O'Connell, Bill White, Dick Pratt, Mario Petersen, Elaine Jacobsen, Joe Rose, and Lee Morse were just a few of them. That was during the week. On the weekends I still got to work with all the pilots I had been working and flying with before. As Alpha Company 3rd of the 126th, we went through a few commanders until we were finally blessed with Captain Rich Clark, a West Point graduate and one of the smartest commanders I have ever had. Judy was moving on and up. I used to say she was the only female who had the brains and the balls to back it up. She was incredibly smart and thorough. This afforded me the great fortune to then work with Steve Shaw. Steve would be the first to admit his computer skills were weak, but as a readiness NCO, he knew the enlisted side of the house, and that in itself was huge. We worked well together, both in-house and out.

On a side note, I had just been assigned to be Alpha Company Commander. There have been only a handful of warrant officers who have served as Company Commander. It was usually a commissioned officer position. I was worried I might be in over my head. I had come to believe, however, that if a leader takes care of his men, they will, in turn, take care of him. I had their collective backs and felt that they had mine.

Steve was my right-hand man during my eighteen months as commander, and he orchestrated the best "thank you" a commander has ever seen. One day, Steve and I were talking about one of my first loves, the Boston Red Sox. During a salary dispute among the players, I happened to mention in passing to Steve that I would pay the Red Sox to let me play left field at Fenway Park. Steve secretly went around and collected money from everybody, and they sent my wife Mary and me to the Red Sox fantasy camp in Florida. It was like a dream come true. I never would have splurged on myself like that. Without a doubt, it was a once-in-a-lifetime experience.

Prior to going to the fantasy camp, I thought I was in pretty good shape. After two days, the only part of my body that didn't hurt was my hair. It was truly one of the greatest thrills of my life. What a great group of guys they were.

[44]

OIF

IN MARCH OF 2005, Operation Iraqi Freedom was foremost on everyone's mind, and we knew as a unit we would be deployed soon. I wasn't sure how to tell Mary, but at some point the orders would come, and I would have to tell her. Mary used to make me lunch every day for work at the National Guard. I had thought about saying to her one day, "Honey, you don't have to make me lunch tomorrow, as I'm off to Iraq," but Tammy Debonise, the surrogate mother to all of us, a buxom blonde, who was the administrative assistant for the facility, said that was crazy. "If it came to that," she said, "I will tell her." Well, the orders had been down for a while, and I put it off as long as I could before I told her. The surprise was on me. She had figured it out a couple of months earlier.

Dwight had elected to retire from the Guard before the deployment, which left Geoff and me as the two token old guys. After serving in my AGR capacity for the last five years and being Company Commander, there was no way I could leave those people and just say, "Tell me how it is when you get home." At first, Geoff had his doubts about going, but the lure of tax-free money was too big a draw to ignore.

We were going to Kuwait for a deployment of fifteen months. My first reaction was, "Kuwait? What are we doing in Kuwait? There's no war in Kuwait!" I thought, "What purpose could we serve in Kuwait?" I was partially right. There wasn't much of a purpose, but it did give pilots the opportunity to fly more and therefore learn more by flying almost every day.

It was during this deployment that I earned the nickname, "short fuse." I butted heads with a lot of people who outranked me. I know that seems out of the norm, but basically I felt that I had achieved the highest rank I could, so what was the worst they could do, send me home? Judy Halstead always said if it was too stupid, we weren't doing it, so I took a page from her playbook. My primary job, in addition to flying, was as the scheduler of the pilots for the assigned missions. In the beginning, everyone wanted to fly. I felt it was more important to have the Alpha Company personnel fly the bulk of the missions first in order to get familiar with the area of operations. People from outside the company would come to me and demand to fly. I earned the name "short fuse" because, after a while, I would lose it and say something like, "This is not a sprint but a marathon. I'll get to all of you as the level of everyone around you progresses."

I butted heads with people who had power, but I had the future in mind. In those confines, it is the *soldiers* who make a deployment. Although we never faced grave danger, we still needed an attitude that said, "We're all in this together," and with a few minor adjustments along the way, we all were.

Nothing of any significance happened during this deployment. It was more about getting through the fifteen months without anyone getting hurt or killing each other. Even in this environment, though, the bonds of brothers in arms is almost mystifying. Initially, there were eight of us living in a twenty-by-twenty-foot room, sleeping in bunk beds with barely enough room to move. We got along as one big BFF fest. We watched shows on DVD late into the night, told stories, and then finally went to sleep, only to get up maybe four or five hours later to go fly a mission.

11—Some of the Band of Brothers in Kuwait

In Vietnam, Al Gore hadn't invented the internet yet, so keeping in touch was done by mail, tape recorders or—if you got lucky—a short-wave radio. Communication was much different in Kuwait. Some units could buy a satellite dish and have internet access. Our unit actually had a phone that allowed us to talk to our facility back home. We could make a call and once connected with the States they connected us to our family. The entire process in Vietnam might take weeks, in Kuwait, it could be minutes.

I think there was good and bad to the situation. On one hand, we could reassure our families that everything was all right. On the other hand, we could be bogged down with information that might distract our attention from our immediate situation. I know it was a comfort for my wife to know how things were going, but I saw some guys walk away from the phone shaking their heads, trying to deal with a situation 6,000 miles away.

While I was deployed, my mom was in a nursing home, and it was just a matter of time before she passed. In the Chasson family, we have a somewhat humorous tradition in the way we tell someone that a person has died. It's a little sick perhaps, but in the right circumstance it works. The joke it's based on goes like this: A travelling salesman is getting ready to go off on a trip. He gives his kids hugs and kisses, says goodbye to his wife, and picks up his cat, Fluffy, who has been with him almost twenty years, and smothers him with all kinds of affection. He tells his wife he will check in with her in a few days, and off he goes. A few days later, he calls home to see how everyone is doing, and his wife tells him that Fluffy is dead. He is stunned by this news. The cat that meant so much to him is dead, and the news of the death is such a shock.

"Honey," he says to his wife, "did you have to tell me that news in such a blunt manner? Couldn't you have softened the blow a little bit by telling me Fluffy got out of the house, and the next thing you know he climbed a tree, then from there onto the roof, from which he then fell off and died—anything to prepare me for the worst?"

His wife apologizes profusely, saying that she wished she had done it his way, and that she is so sorry. The husband, still in disbelief, says he has to hang up, but promises he will call in a few days.

A few days later he calls and says, "Hi, honey, how is everything?"

To which the wife replies, "Your mom is on the roof."

That is exactly what Matt and my roommates said to me. I hadn't even remembered telling Matt this joke. It was late at night, and I was just getting ready for bed when Matt and the rest of my roommates came up to my bunk, and he said, "Wayne, your mom's on the roof." Only from a Chasson—or Matt Cummings—could that have worked so effectively. But that's exactly how my mom would have wanted me to get the news.

As a group, we all went outside—me, to reflect on my great mom, and the guys to be there for me if I needed them. I had never seen any birds in Kuwait, but that night, standing with the guys, a huge flock of white birds took to the sky, and I felt my mother's spirit. I went home on emergency leave. I was home for a week to pay my respects and be with family. It was great to be able to see the family, but sad to say goodbye to my mom. Then it was back to the desert to be with my other family.

Traveling back and forth on emergency leave, I was struck with the drastic contrast between this experience and my Vietnam days. In Vietnam, any attention we got when traveling back and forth on commercial airlines was negative. The exact opposite was the case during Operation Iraqi Freedom. We were always thanked for our service by airline employees and passengers alike and upgraded if possible to first class. I felt a little uncomfortable with this attention. It was a drastic difference than my previous travels. Don't get me wrong, it was welcomed but still hard to justify in my mind. I do remember on my first return that my wife, Mary, was able to meet me at the gate. We fell into each other's arms with such a collision that I thought we might both fall over in front of everyone deplaning. If only for a week or so we would be together again, a memory of which I will cherish forever.

Arriving home from the desert when the deployment was over was an adjustment. We had been away fifteen months, and now that we were back on Cape Cod, the flying environment was totally different. In Kuwait and Iraq, we never did instrument flying, it was strictly visual. We needed to re-learn our instrument skills, especially with the fog on Cape Cod that could, and very often did, materialize out of nowhere. We got back from deployment around mid-November, and our first scheduled drill was not until February.

I was back at my full-time AGR job the first week of December because I had used up all my leave time due to two deaths in the family—Mary's father had passed away as well. A mission came up in February in which the Massachusetts state adjutant general needed to be picked up at state headquarters in Milford and brought to the Cape for a meeting. I was assigned the mission, along with C.J. Turgeon, a pilot, and Pete Gamelin, the crew chief. The weather on the Cape can sometimes be zero visibility, while just on the other side of the canal it can be "clear blue and 22." The weather that Sunday was foggy, and although the clouds and ceiling were low, the visibility was pretty good.

I checked the weather and was given an okay forecast on the Cape, and beautiful weather off Cape. I even called the general's aide to ask how the weather was up in Milford. He responded, "It's beautiful up here, chief."

I sat down with C.J. and Pete and went over what the mission and the weather was. All were comfortable with the plan. I even called the weather one more time as we were walking out the door and still had a green light. We had one more re-brief at the aircraft on what we could expect and what we would do if the weather wasn't acceptable. We climbed in, started the engines, and got ready for takeoff. I had a habit of having two of my radios dialed into the instrument approach at Otis and approach control, in addition to the normal tower frequency. If anything went wrong, I didn't want to be looking down at the radios and trying to dial the appropriate frequencies.

We took off and had about 500 feet of ceiling. We progressed a little further, but the ceiling was dropping to the point that we were maybe a hundred feet off the trees. I knew the area route, having flown it hundreds of times before. We were close to the canal, and I thought, *Clear blue and 22 is just a half a mile away.* Just then, C.J. said, "I've lost the ground."

Pete yelled, "I've still got it." Not for long though, as just a few seconds later, we'd all lost the ground.

At this point, in aviation safety, there were two things we could do. One was to try and lower the helicopter to pick up ground references, the other was to go up into the clouds, adjust from visual reference to instrument reference, and rely on our training and skills. The problem was we hadn't done any instrument-based flying in the last fifteen months—none at all.

C.J. started a climb into the clouds at an angle that was a little too steep. To correct for this, he nosed the aircraft over. This can be the start of vertigo, and an "oh shit" moment. I was still talking C.J. through the inadvertent weather situation, and the next thing I thought I heard was Pete Gamelin saying, "We're gonna die, we're gonna die."

I said, "No we're not," and, with my left hand on the cyclic, started to right the helicopter. I used my left hand, which you usually don't do, because my right hand was flipping the switch to call the tower and approach. We leveled off, and C.J. had the helicopter under control as I was talking to tower. Tower switched us to approach control and asked, "Do we want to declare an emergency?"

I said, "No," thinking things were fine now.

The approach operator came back and said, "Are you instrument qualified?"

I replied, "Yes, but it's been fifteen months, so give me your best man."

C.J. did a beautiful instrument approach where we broke out of the clouds just at the minimum altitude for the landing. I called the general to tell him his ride wasn't going to happen, and he said, "No worries, chief." Making us look good, the weather never improved at all the rest of the day.

After incidents of any nature that I thought were important, I would always have a de-brief and look at what had just happened to see if we could have done things differently. So, the three of us talked and decided there was nothing that we should have done instead of what we did do. We relied on our training to get out of an "oh shit" moment. I did have an analogy for this kind of incident, however: Going blind by surprise into the clouds is a little like jumping into the deep end of a very cold pool of water with your clothes on. At first, there is the initial shock of the cold, which almost takes your breath away. Then there's the struggle of swimming with all your clothes on. If you just relax for thirty seconds and catch your breath, you can adjust to the situation and swim to the edge of the pool. We laughed about what Pete had said in the aircraft, but he was quick to point out that what he said was, "We're in a dive, we're in a dive." It sure sounded like, "We're gonna die, we're gonna die."

[45]

CASUALTY ASSISTANCE

OFFICER

PROBABLY THE MOST memorable, challenging, and frightening experience that I ever had while in the AGR program was when I was designated as a casualty assistance officer (CAO). When a soldier dies due to any circumstances while on active duty, the Army notifies their next of kin. The days of using the telegram for notification ended long ago. These days, a casualty notification officer (CNO) follows specific procedures when notifying a family. There is nothing more painful than knocking at the door of a family member to tell them their son or daughter has died. The officer is in uniform and, if lucky enough, is accompanied by a local chaplain, minister, or priest. The next day, a CAO comes to talk to the family about what the Army will and can do to help during this emotional time.

I was the CAO for the family of Zach Tellier of Falmouth, Massachusetts. Army Sgt. Zach Tellier died September 29, 2007, while serving during Operation Enduring Freedom in Afghanistan. He was thirty-one. The day after the initial notification by CNO Major Bob O'Connell, it was my job to go to the house and talk to his family. Their family circumstances were perhaps not that unusual but could have presented the potential for some awkward moments. Zach, from Falmouth, married a girl from New Hampshire who, at the time of his death, was living in North Carolina. His parents were divorced. The father had remarried and was living northwest of Boston, and his mom was in Falmouth. Major O'Connell offered to go to the house of Zach's mom with me, where everyone was waiting for us. We had a scheduled teleconference call with the wife in North Carolina.

Understandably, everyone was in shock and denial. I had faced many a situation in my life that scared the daylights out of me, but none as scary as this. Steve Shaw, my readiness NCO, had been assigned the same task with another family and tried to give me all the "dos" and "don'ts," but there really is no preparation for something like that. We helped the family plan a memorial that all involved seemed to agree would have been in accordance with Zach's wishes and good for the family. A contingent of soldiers from Fort Bragg was supposed to take care of Zach's widow. I was to concentrate on his mother and father. Somehow, the contingent from North Carolina left everything to me. I thought they would be better at the arrangements, but they said I was doing a great job. I had no idea what I was doing, I was just going by feel.

With the help of the full-time staff at the Otis facility, and even my wife Mary driving people around, it was a truly moving ceremony from the minute Zach's casket arrived at Otis all the way up until Taps and a flyby of Black Hawk helicopters. Zach's parents were so grateful to me, but it was *them* who helped *me* to relax, and just honor their son.

[46]

JROTC WAREHAM AND

THE FINAL FLIGHT

I WAS APPROACHING the Guard's new mandatory retirement age of sixty-two when an opportunity came up for a teaching position at Wareham High School in the JROTC program. The pay was supposed to be comparable to what I was making as a W4 in the Army. I had to decide whether I should take a job teaching, which I had enjoyed before, and retire one year early, or stay in the AGR job and hope that something would come up when I had to retire at sixty-two. I chose the teaching position. I made my announcement only a few weeks before my actual departure date. I didn't want a big goodbye. I just wanted to slip out the back door.

We arranged a final flight on the Saturday of drill weekend, with five Black Hawk helicopters prepped and ready. I was to fly with Matt Cummings in the lead helicopter, and I had the route of flight all planned out. We took off from Otis and headed towards Hyannis, MA, flying down the coast at approximately 500 feet. We called Hyannis tower, asked for a low approach, and we veered slightly east to fly over my old restaurant and then on to Hyannis Port Golf Club where I was still a longtime member. From there, we headed to Boston, where I intended to just fly through the city from the south and exit to the west.

We had to call the tower at Logan Airport in order to ask for permission to enter their airspace. The female tower operator said, "Bosox two-three, stand by." (Bosox two-three was my call sign while flying in the Black Hawks.) A male tower operator came on the radio and said, "Bosox two-three, this is Boston Tower."

I answered, "This is Bosox two-three, go."

He asked, "Is this Wayne Chasson?"

I was stunned. I looked around as though there was a hidden camera or something—how did he know it was me?

I replied, "Affirmative."

He said something like, "Would you mind doing a low approach down 04 Left, so we in the tower can salute you and your thirty years of flying?"

I was still in shock when Matt told me the pilots and crew had gotten together and called Boston tower ahead of the flight, so he knew we were coming. We were chugging along at 150 knots or so, passing all these commercial airline jets burning fuel and time just waiting on me. The pilots in the commercial jets could hear my conversation with the tower, and when the tower operator mentioned Vietnam, I thought, "Wow, this is so exciting for me," and I hoped it was for all the other crews in the flight. We then headed towards Fenway Park so I could have one last flyover. As we headed back to the Cape, I tried to fly over every crewmember's house or town as a way of saying "thank you" to them.

The flight ended back at Otis with all aircraft in an in-echelon formation, peeling off one-by-one. I was the last to land. As we taxied up, my family was there with the drill weekend crowd and a fire truck. My daughter Emily hosed me down as everyone cheered. It was quite an honor to have flown with a great crew, and to have everyone there to say goodbye. Two days later, I started my first day at Wareham High School.

I mention this as much as anything for the mere fact that one day I was flying and doing something I knew well. Two days later, I was teaching a program I knew nothing about. There were lesson plans and the latest technology to master in my new endeavor, but nothing really prepared me for working with kids age fifteen to nineteen. Believe me, there is a world of difference between a fifth-grade student and a high school student. Everything was totally different from my experience before. Plus, I was replacing a JROTC instructor who had been with the students the previous three years. It took many hours of nightly preparation to be ready for the next day. I would be at school ten hours a day, then spend five hours at night preparing. At first I thought I had made the biggest mistake of my life, but with the help of the staff, specifically Kristy, Henry, Sue, Meagan, Judy, and of course Sherri, I slowly succeeded.

[47]

ONE MORE DANCE . . .

PLEASE

O NE LESSON PLAN that I tailored to the students concerning their future career choices was something that I later took to heart. I told my students there were three ways to go to work: First, you *have* to go work; second, you *want* to go to work; and third, you *get* to go to work. Working at a job where you can honestly say, "I *get* to go to work and get paid," is the most rewarding way to go through life.

It was this philosophy that inspired me, after teaching four years at Wareham High School, to think, "What the heck," and submit an application to Evergreen Helicopters after seeing an employment ad to fly the Puma helicopter in Afghanistan. It was a full year later when Evergreen Helicopters called me and asked, "Are you still interested in the open position?"

I thought about the risks involved and decided "Yes. I want to fly again." Evergreen Helicopters was bought by Erickson Helicopters, but I still had my chance at flying again.

12—Our call sign with Erikson

Even at the tender age of sixty-seven, I felt lucky to still *get* to go to work. For almost three years I worked on a six-week rotation schedule, back and forth from Afghanistan to my home on Cape Cod. My arrival in Afghanistan was nothing like my arrival in Vietnam had been. In one respect I was a grizzled veteran with a lot of combat hours under my belt. Yet I was still a rookie, having just learned a new aircraft, and was unsure as to what was going to happen next or even where would I be going.

In my first week of flying Evergreen/Erickson Helicopters in Afghanistan, I had several missions that took me into different Forward Operating Bases (or FOBs). Each base had a name which might represent the local village or a soldier who had been killed from the unit that supported that base. The pilots I was flying with were from all over the world and would pronounce the names of these firebases differently each time we went in. One day, while waiting for personnel to get on the helicopter in a FOB, I noticed a sign where we had landed that said in big letters, "Welcome to FOB Tellier." It was named after Zach Tellier, the soldier I had served as casualty affairs officer for. But because of the butchered English, I never realized it was in honor of Zach until I saw it in print. I thought it was only fitting that all these years later I should end up where Zach's life had ended.

My living quarters were at FOB Shank, about forty miles south of Kabul. Upon arrival I was assigned a small cubicle in an eight-man tent, sectioned off by some plywood. When I asked where my cubicle was located, the answer was, "Yours is the one next to the one that was hit by a rocket day before yesterday." As I settled into my new room I noticed one of my walls was peppered with bits of shrapnel. I learned that the day before, one of our great South African mechanics was talking to his wife via FaceTime when an incoming rocket hit the tent next door. He was hit by shrapnel, which his wife only partially witnessed, but thankfully his injuries were not life-threatening.

My first thought was, *Here we go again!* and my second thought was, *Could the Viet Cong have told the Taliban I was coming?* I decided to go with the idea that lightning doesn't strike in the same place twice. It was all the consolation I had.

THIS "BAND OF BROTHERS" was not quite like it had been in my previous aviation experiences. The people I flew and worked with were close, but because we rotated out every six weeks or so it just wasn't the same. The flight managers were an incredible bunch of guys though. Mostly South Africans, they brought a genuine caring to their occupation, and if you ever want a personal CrossFit trainer, Lou Van Wyk and Chris Oertel are pure torture. The flight engineers were some of the most hardworking, dedicated mechanics I had ever been around. They always had a smile on their faces, no matter how long the day. Every day I trusted them with my life, and every day they brought me home. The fellow pilots I flew with had their egos. Some were dickheads, some were control freaks, and a few were even both, but all were professional.

For the most part, it was still us against them. Some things never change. A few of our aircraft had been hit by ground fire, but nobody was a "magnet-ass." Our biggest concerns were the daily incoming rocket attacks. Unlike in Vietnam, we had an early warning system. We had approximately two seconds to hear the warning, hit the ground in a prone position, and hope for the best. At FOB Shank, it was a daily occurrence, happening anywhere from 3 p.m. to 6 p.m. There was no defense for it. Everyone thought, *When your time is up, your time is up*. It got to the point where I would keep my finger on the mute button if I was talking to Mary on FaceTime, so she couldn't hear all the commotion. I would try and time my conversations with her well before or after the predictable rocket attacks. This worked pretty well, except for one time. I think she had a pretty good idea of what was going on, but if we didn't talk about it, then we could pretend it wasn't happening.

Our living quarters resembled my previous overseas conditions—a small cubicle six-feet-by-eight-feet that you made as comfortable as possible for the next six weeks. You couldn't do much in the way of DIY projects because on rotation someone was taking your spot and you had no idea if you would be in the same location on your return.

The Winters were cold as expected, but what I didn't expect was the heat in some areas. In Jalalabad the elevation was approximately 1,800 feet. In Kabul it was 5,500 feet. This might not seem like much of a difference but in the summer the temperature in Jalalabad would reach 125 degrees on a regular basis. Combine that temperature while sitting on the airfield tarmac inside a glass cockpit with all your protective gear on and it was probably close to 140 degrees inside the cockpit. Your vision was partially obscured from the sweat dripping down your forehead. This might rival Robin Williams declaration of "Africa Hot" from the movie *Good Morning Vietnam*.

13—In the pilot's seat in Afghanistan

IN CONCLUSION

AT THE INSISTENCE of my step-daughter Kate and "German," a flight engineer with Erickson whom I trust with my life, I decided to put my memories of the past six decades down on paper. I just started doodling, and the next thing I knew I had page after page. I would jot down notes on some of the longer legs in Afghanistan, and at night try to make sense out of the scribbles. I don't know for sure, but I'm pretty confident that time fades all memories and most of the hurt. If there was anything negative to hold onto, I've tried to let it go. People and places have gotten distorted. Things that were "oh shit" moments have ended up being funny anecdotes years later.

In the past I tried not to tell any war stories, per se. No, "So there I was, all alone, surrounded by a hundred Viet Cong," or some such thing. Sometimes at annual training in the National Guard, Dwight, Geoff, and I might get started on some stories, or over a few beers someone might say something that will give me a bit of a flashback and I'll mention it, but not very often. If I do have a story, I try to make it short and at least a bit humorous. In the National Guard there were others with stories to tell, and mine didn't seem that unique. Returning from Vietnam it was almost better to hide the fact that I had been in the Army than to share any of my stories or emotions. To the civilian population, I didn't think anyone would be interested or would even understand the technical aspects of what I was trying to convey in just a few short sentences. Four individuals who did seem genuinely interested were Peter Vandermark, Leslie Kerr, Rick Jurgens, and my wife Mary, who was always interested and has heard more than a few stories but now, with this memoir, she gets all of them. I could tell by looking into their eyes that what I had to say in those moments had an effect on them.

One reason that I wanted to write about this part of my life was so that someday, when I'm really old and start to forget things, I will have something to help me remember that part of my life. Another reason was because I want Meagan, Katie, Emily, Kate, Bobby, and my grandchildren to have an idea of what I was like as a twenty-year-old.

Meagan, my oldest, is the unexpected wonderful gift from a very short lived relationship. Katie and Emily are my bright and funny hard-working daughters from my many years of marriage to Maureen. Kate and Bobby are Mary's children and have now been my step-children for the twenty years we have been married. Together we have all formed our own version of "family," and I consider myself a very lucky man.

My flying career ended after six decades—a seventh is definitely out of the question. If I can't laugh looking back at six decades of flying, I can at least smile when I think of the people I've met and some of the things that have happened to me. I still to this day wonder, "How in the world did I not die?" That must have been "the plan" all along.

When communicating by radio in Vietnam or in the National Guard, our query and response was usually, "Such-and-such, this is Minuteman two-three [or Musket three-two], over." That would initiate the conversation. When the conversation was finished and there was no need for any additional dialogue, I would say, "This is Minuteman two-three [or Musket three-two, Bosox two-three], out" –

which would signal the end of the conversation.

So, since that about says it all, I will end with, "This is Minuteman two-three, OUT."

ACKNOWLEDGEMENTS

THERE ARE SO many people to thank for encouraging me to write my memoirs. There are the obvious ones who supported me and were willing to listen. There are my brothers in arms, the everyday pilots and crews that I flew with, those bands of brothers who trusted me to bring them back and those that I trusted to help me see that through—too endless to name but all of those from Vietnam, the Guard soldiers from Iraq, Kuwait, and Afghanistan.

My immediate and extended family: Meagan, Katie, Emily, Kate, and Bobby. They will learn some things that I never shared, too afraid to bore them, yet they were always willing to listen if I had been willing to talk.

Especially to Kate and German, who gently kept pushing and confidently encouraging me to even start the memoirs.

Thanks to Ed Eubanks for the initial edit, and Paul who edited the images. Of course there is Mary, my wife. She never gave up on me. She was my first proofreader, not to mention the second, third, and fourth proofreader and my biggest cheerleader. Anne Brazel was my quality relief specialist who gave the manuscript a once over, and Erin Cummings was my closer. Special thinks to Phil Catchings. Phil was the consummate professional advising, correcting, resequencing essentially just about everything to make *This is Minuteman* a reality. To Margaret Diehl, who worked her magic to allow me to feel that's how I wanted my story told. Had I printed the manuscript in what I thought was the final draft I would have been embarrassed. And to Rodney Miles, one person who really felt there was something here, hidden perhaps, but he shaped it and brought *This is Minuteman* to life on a professional level.

So many to thank, so many stories probably untold, but they will remain in my heart and memory forever.

Each chapter of my flying career was unique with the men I served. Whether it was sharing the dangers of Vietnam, the camaraderie and tribulations of my National Guard brothers, or the men and mayhem of Afghanistan, they *all* made this story possible. And for that I thank each and every one of you.

HISTORY OF THE HUEY

THE FIRST FLIGHT of the Huey was piloted by Floyd Carlson on October 22, 1956, in Fort Worth, Texas. The UH-1 helicopter has logged over 27,000,000 flight hours since that date. Together, the Huey and the Cobra have more combat hours flown than any other aircraft in the history of warfare. Records indicate that of the 7,013 Hueys that served in the Vietnam War, almost all of those were with the Army.

1,925 Hueys were lost to combat, while 1,380 were lost in operational accidents. These high losses reflect their heavy use rather than a fragility of the aircraft—and heavy use leading to crew fatigue contributed to the high accident rate. Huey aircraft casualties (those killed in action) include the loss of 1,074 pilots and 1,103 aircrew members. Vietnam has been called the "first helicopter war," and the Huey remains a symbol of the conflict, far more than any other weapon. The Huey remains a legend as the most successful rotorcraft in aviation history.

BELL UH-1H HUEY[3]

---

[3] Developed into. Bell AH-1 Cobra. Bell 214. The Bell UH-1 Iroquois (nicknamed "Huey") is a utility military helicopter powered by a single turboshaft engine, with two-blade main and tail rotors. — Wikipedia

US ARMY UTILITY AIRCRAFT

Range:	250NM
Cruise Speed:	90KTS
Max Speed:	124KTS
Service Ceiling:	14,500 FT
Engine Lycoming:	T53-L-13
Shaft Power:	1,125 SHP
Empty Weight:	7,184 LBS
Max Weight:	9,500 LBS
External Load:	2,000 LBS
Crew:	2 Pilots
	2 Gunners
	9 Troops

THE WALL

ALL GAVE SOME, SOME GAVE ALL

A LITTLE HISTORY most people will never know, along with some personal reflections (with several references from http://thewall-usa.com/names.asp):

- There are 58,267 names now listed on that polished black wall, including those added in 2010.

- The names are arranged in the order in which they were taken from us by date, and within each date the names are alphabetized. It is hard to believe it has been over sixty years since the first casualty.

- The first known casualty was Richard B. Fitzgibbon, of North Weymouth, Massachusetts, listed by the U.S. Department of Defense as having been killed on June 8, 1956. His name is listed on the Wall with that of his son, Marine Corps Lance Cpl. Richard B. Fitzgibbon III, who was killed on Sept. 7, 1965.

- There are three sets of fathers and sons on the Wall.

- Thirty-nine thousand, nine hundred and ninety-seven on the Wall were just twenty-two or younger. Eight thousand two hundred and eighty-three were just nineteen years old.

- The largest age group, 33,103 were eighteen years old.

- Twelve soldiers on the Wall were seventeen years old. Five soldiers on the Wall were sixteen years old.

- One soldier, PFC Dan Bullock was fifteen years old.

- Nine hundred ninety-seven soldiers were killed on their first day in Vietnam.

- Fourteen hundred forty-eight soldiers were killed on what was supposed to be their last day in Vietnam.

- Thirty-one sets of brothers are on the Wall. Thirty-one sets of parents lost two of their sons.

- Fifty-four soldiers attended Thomas Edison High School in Philadelphia. I wonder why so many from one school.

- Eight women are on the Wall, who died nursing the wounded.

- Two hundred and forty-four soldiers were awarded the Medal of Honor during the Vietnam War; 153 of them are on the Wall.

- Beallsville, Ohio, with a population of 475, lost six of her sons.

- West Virginia had the highest casualty rate per capita in the nation. There are 711 West Virginians on the Wall.

- The Marines of Morenci led some of the scrappiest high school football and basketball teams that the little Arizona Copper town of Morenci (pop. 5,058) had ever known and cheered. They enjoyed roaring beer busts. In quieter moments, they rode horses along the Coronado Trail, stalking deer in the Apache National Forest. In the patriotic camaraderie typical of Morenci's mining families, the nine graduates of Morenci High enlisted as a group in the Marine Corps. Their service began on Independence Day, 1966. Only three returned home.

- The Buddies of Midvale—LeRoy Tafoya, Jimmy Martinez, Tom Gonzales—were all boyhood friends and lived on three consecutive streets in Midvale, Utah—Fifth, Sixth and Seventh Avenues. They lived only a few yards apart and played together at the adjacent sandlot ball field. And they all went to Vietnam. In a span of sixteen dark days in late 1967, all three would be killed. LeRoy was killed on Wednesday, November 22, the fourth anniversary of John F. Kennedy's assassination. Jimmy died less than twenty-four hours later on Thanksgiving Day. Tom was shot dead assaulting the enemy on Dec. 7, Pearl Harbor Remembrance Day.

- The most casualty deaths for a single day were on January 31, 1968: 245 deaths.

- The most casualty deaths for a single month were May 1968: 2,415 casualties were incurred.

- Most Americans who read this will only see the numbers that the Vietnam War created. To those of us who survived the war, and to the families of those who did not, we see the faces and feel the pain that these numbers created.

- We are—until we, too, pass away—haunted with these numbers, because they were our friends, fathers, husbands, wives, sons and daughters. There are no noble wars, just noble warriors.

- More than 58,000 Americans and at least 1.5 million Vietnamese died in the war that divided the country as nothing else had done since the American Civil War.

Glossary/Term Quick Reference

105s — refers to 105mm Howitzer M3 cannon rounds, used by artillery units as well as infantry as a light-duty artillery cannon.

155s — refers to the M114 155mm Howitzer, a medium-duty artillery cannon; see also "105s" above.

1S/1A Draft Status — part of the classification system used by the U.S. military to designate status of eligible draftees. "1A" was "available" while "1S" was classified as a "student deferred [from the draft] by statute."

A-4 — the Douglas A-4 Skyhawk was a single-seat lightweight jet that could carry missiles, bombs, or other munitions. It was a key part of the air military strategy during the Vietnam War.

A-6 — the Grumman A-6 Intruder was a medium-weight, carrier-based attack craft used by the U.S. Navy and Marine Corps. It was an "all-weather" aircraft, meaning it was adapted for use at night or during other times of bad visibility.

Aircraft Commander — Head pilot in command of the aircraft and all decision-making responsibilities of mission.

AK-47 — also known as the Kalashnikov, this is a Russian-made, selective-fire (meaning it could be set to automatic or semi-automatic) 7.62mm assault rifle. It was the weapon of choice for the Viet Cong and North Vietnamese, and in the author's estimation just about the best automatic rifle ever made. The AK-47 was tough and resilient, able to be buried in mud and still come out firing.

AO – Area of Operations, the region where combat took place for a particular attack.

Article 15 – a form of non-judicial punishment authorized by article fifteen of the Uniform Code of Military Justice, which permits commanding officers to administratively discipline troops without a court-martial.

Battalion – a military unit in the U.S. Army composed of a headquarters and two or more batteries, companies, or troops.

(The) Bear – Wayne's nickname given to him by the "band of brothers" during WOC training.

Black Hawk – see "UH-60."

Brigade – a military unit in the U.S. Army composed of several battalions; it is considered to be a major tactical formation.

CA – Combat Assault, the insertion of troops by helicopter transport.

Candidate – an enlisted soldier who is enrolled in the Army's Warrant Officer Career College and is considered to be on track to become a warrant officer but has not yet earned his warrant.

CAP – "combined action platoon," a unit of the Combined Action Program, one of the most effective counter-insurgency efforts implemented during the Vietnam War.

CH-54 – the Sikorsky CH-54 Tarhe "sky-crane" helicopter was used in the Vietnam War for transport and downed-aircraft retrieval. It could carry a payload of up to 20,000 pounds, and did not need to land to deliver or recover objects but could winch them up and down while airborne.

Charlie – see Viet Cong.

Charlie model – the Bell UH-1C, a variation of the Huey.

Chicken plate – a type of body armor commonly worn by aviators, capable of defeating large-caliber armor-piercing rounds.

Clear blue and 22 – aviation slang meaning clear skies; twenty-two refers to visibility, in terms of miles.

Cobra – the Bell AH-1 Cobra is a variation of the "Huey" family of helicopters; it was the backbone of the Army's attack helicopter fleet until it was replaced by the AH-64 Apache. It flew with a simplified crew of two, with a single pilot and a co-pilot/gunner, and was typically armed with grenade launchers and/or mini-guns and 2.75in/70mm rockets.

Company – a military unit in the U.S. Army that is typically composed of three platoons and usually commanded by a captain (though sometimes a major or a first lieutenant).

Corps – a military unit in the U.S. Army composed of several divisions.

CS Grenade – a grenade loaded with the chemical compound 2-chlorobenzalmalononitrile, the primary component in tear gas; it is commonly used as a riot-control agent. The compound was discovered by Ben Corson and Roger Stoughton in 1928, and the name is derived from the first letters of their surnames.

Deacon – John Biddar's nickname given to him by the "band of brothers" in WOCC.

DEROS – an acronym for "date of expected return from overseas"; the date a soldier was shipped home.

Deuce and a half – the M35, medium-duty, ten-wheel cargo truck used by the military for many years; the moniker comes from its two-and-a-half-ton rating.

Didi Mau – Vietnamese for "move out as fast as you can."

Dinks – Viet Cong and NVA

Dinky Dau – Vietnamese for "crazy."

Division – a military unit in the U.S. Army composed of several regiments or brigades.

Donut Dollies – women who voluntarily traveled to Vietnam to provide entertainment and distractions for the troops during warfare.

Drill Instructor – any of the non-commissioned officers charged with the task of indoctrinating new recruits who enter the U.S. military.

Drill Sergeant – the particular category of drill instructor for the U.S. Army. The sergeant ranks above privates, private-first-class, specialists, and corporals. Sergeants wear an insignia of three chevrons.

F-4 – the McDonnell Douglas F-4 Phantom is a dual-seat, long-range supersonic fighter-bomber, capable of carrying more than 18,000 pounds of munitions including air-to-air and air-to-ground missiles and various bombs. Along with the A-4, the F-4 was a major element of air military strategy throughout the Vietnam War.

Fire Team – A gunship team of two aircraft.

Flying Tiger Airlines – the transport planes that carried troops from the U.S. to Vietnam.

Freedom Bird – Any airplane that took American soldiers back to the U.S. at the end of their tour of duty.

Getting short – a slang term indicating that someone's tour of duty was almost completed; usually this meant that they had thirty days or less left before they would go home.

Gooks – see Viet Cong.

Helmet – the nickname of one of Wayne's "band of brothers" from WOCC.

Hooch – a term for the plywood huts that housed the aviators in the base camp in Vietnam.

Hooch Maids – local Vietnamese women who tended to the aviators' quarters in the base camp.

Huey – See UH-1.

IFR – Instrument flight rules, which is the set of regulations guiding how a pilot would fly when flight by visual reference is unsafe.

IMC – Instrument Meteorological Conditions; weather conditions that require pilots to fly primarily by reference to instruments.

JG Willis – a company in Watertown, MA, that makes and rents commercial-grade tents.

(The) Judge – the nickname given to one of Wayne's "band of brothers" in WOCC.

KIAs – Killed in Action.

Kit Carson Scouts – former Viet Cong combatants who had switched sides and were used as intelligence scouts for the U.S. forces in Vietnam.

Klick – an abbreviation-word for "kilometer" in the military.

KP – kitchen patrol, more formally known as mess duty, which is sometimes assigned as punishment for a minor infraction and thus is considered to be an undesirable assignment.

Laagering – making camp.

Loach – see OH-6.

LZ – landing zone.

M-14 – a .308-caliber automatic rifle that was standard-issue for military personnel from 1961 (replacing the M-1 Garand) until 1970 (when it was replaced by the M-16).

M-60 – a general-purpose, 7.62mm "machine gun" (meaning it fires cartridges from a disintegrating belt, rather than from a magazine); it was frequently mounted on a pintle in the doors of helicopters, but sometimes mounted or held using other methods when firing from a helicopter.

Medevac Missions – medical evacuations or missions conducted under the premise of a medical emergency, evacuating wounded troops from an LZ.

Minuteman – the "call sign" for any member of the "slicks" in the

176th Assault Helicopter Company.

Muff – the nickname for Bruce Riddle in the "band of brothers" in WOCC.

Musket – the "call sign" for any member of the gunship platoon in the 176th Assault Helicopter Company.

NVA – the People's Army of Vietnam, commonly referred to as the North Vietnamese Army.

OH-6 – the Hughes OH-6 Cayuse is a light operation helicopter, or LOH (from which the nickname "Loach" is derived). It carries a crew of two and can be armed with M-60 or M-134 miniguns, .50-cal. MG pods, up to fourteen 2.75in./70mm rockets, and/or four TOW or Hellfire missiles.

OH-13 – the Bell H-13 Sioux, a light observation helicopter which was a single-pilot craft with capacity for two passengers and had a dome-covered cockpit open on the sides.

OH-23 – the Fairchild-Hiller OH-23 Raven, a light observation helicopter, which was piloted by a crew of two and had a dome-covered cockpit open on the sides.

Peter pilot – the second pilot during a learning exercise, who was being instructed by the lead pilot (the Aircraft Commander, or "A/C"). Used to designate a new arrival in the 176th Assault Helicopter Company.

Platoon – a military unit in the U.S. Army composed of a designated number of troops, which is determined by the intended purpose of the platoon. The platoon is frequently organized into sections or squads.

Pop Smoke – to set off a smoke-emitting flare to indicate the location of a unit or group of troops.

Psyops – psychological operations, planned operations designed to influence the opposing forces' emotions, motives, behavior, and reasoning.

PT – physical training, the regimen of activities required of recruits and other soldiers to ensure muscular strength, endurance, and cardiovascular fitness; it normally consists of running, push-ups, sit-ups, calisthenics, the use of obstacle courses, and other rigorous exercises.

Recruit – a term used interchangeably for the rank of "private E-1," which is the lowest rank in the U.S. Army; recruits wear no insignia to indicate their rank.

Regiment – a military unit in the U.S. Army; at the time of the Vietnam War, the Army employed an organizational structure known as the Combat Arms Regimental System (CARS), which utilized regiments as parent organizations for historical purposes, composed of divisions, brigades, and battalions; effectively, the association with a regiment was in name only.

Rockpile – Marine base near the DMZ.

Sapper – generally, a soldier who clears paths, lays and clears land mines, etc. In Wayne's description, they also were assigned "suicide squad" tasks, and were adept at stealth infiltration and attack.

Seabee – a member of the U.S. Naval Construction Forces; the term comes from the initials C.B. (Construction Battalion).

Section – a military unit in the U.S. Army that historically has consisted of a "half-platoon" and sometimes is sub-divided into squads.

Short Final – an aviation term describing the point in the final approach to a landing when final radio clearance for landing is requested by the pilot(s).

Slicks – the slick platoons were the general aviation units, flying helicopters on a wide variety of missions; they were designated in contrast to the gunship platoon, which flew more specialized missions.

Snowbird - Temporary holding status of soon to be pilots waiting for class assignment.

Snuff – the nickname of one of Wayne's "band of brothers" in WOCC.

Squad – a military unit in the U.S. Army that is usually composed of eight to fourteen individual soldiers.

(The) T – the nickname for the Massachusetts Bay Transit Authority and its network of light rail, bus, subway, and ferry lines.

TAC Officer – the common term for the "Training, Advising, and Counseling Officer" employed by one of the Warrant Officer Career Colleges as the primary instructors for candidates.

Triple Canopy – this was the thickest, heaviest vegetation in the jungle, growing at ground, intermediate, and high levels all at once.

UH-1 – the Bell UH-1 Iroquois (unofficially known as a "Huey" because of its original designation as the "HU-1A"), a versatile helicopter commissioned by the U.S. military that could be configured with rocket launchers, grenade launchers, and machine guns along with the capacity to carry up to fourteen troops or six medical stretchers, and could be crewed by a single pilot. For more on the Huey, see the appendix on "The History of the Huey."

UH-60 – the Sikorsky UH-60 Black Hawk helicopter is a medium-duty utility helicopter that, in 1979, replaced the UH-1 Huey as the Army's tactical transport helicopter. As with the Huey, a number of variants are in use; generally, the Black Hawk is similar in function to the Huey, with a crew of two pilots and two crew chiefs/ gunners. It can be armed with machine guns, mini-guns, gatling guns, missiles, rockets, and bombs. In addition to increased speed, weight capacity, and range over the Huey, the Black Hawk is also equipped with advanced electronics and computerized systems.

Viet Cong – the name given by Western sources to the National Liberation Front, a political organization that had organized an army called the People's Liberation Armed Forces of South Vietnam (PLAF). Military forces referred to the Viet Cong by the initials V-C, which were represented in the NATO Phonetic Alphabet as "Victor Charlie;" eventually this was shortened to simply "Charlie." Wayne reflects: "We also called them Charles, Chuck, Victor, Charlie, VC, or dinks."

Wannabes – a moniker for those who "want to be" a warrant officer in the WOCS.

Warrant Officer – an officer in the military who is designated as an officer by warrant, rather than by commission.

Willy Pete – white phosphorus, or WP, munitions were used as tracer rounds to illuminate the path of fire. In NATO phonetic alphabet, WP is stated as William Peter, which is easily shortened to Willy Pete.

Wingman – Second aircraft in the fire team.

WOC – a warrant officer candidate (see Candidate).

WOCS – the U.S. Army's Warrant Officer School, located at Fort Rucker, AL. Similar to OCS.

Zee – the nickname of one of the author's "band of brothers" in WOCC.